He Won Them for Christ

30 Conversions under Spurgeon's Ministry

Eric Hayden

Christian Focus Publications

Dedicated to the memory
of
Harold Griffiths Hayden
my elder brother
whose conversion first attracted me
to Jesus Christ and was the first link in the chain of
my own conversion at the age of twelve.

© Christian Focus Publications Ltd
ISBN 1 85792 059 4

Published in 1993
by
Christian Focus Publications Ltd
Geanies House, Fearn, Ross-shire,
IV20 1TW, Scotland, Great Britain.

Printed and bound in Great Britain
by Cox & Wyman Ltd, Reading, Berkshire

Cover design
by
Donna Macleod

Contents

'When I was told that God had saved a soul
through my ministry ... I felt like a diver who had
been down to the depths of the sea, and *brought up
a rare pearl*' (C H Spurgeon).

INTRODUCTION

I was brought up in a Spurgeonic home. My parents and grandparents had close connections with Spurgeon's Metropolitan Tabernacle and the Stockwell Orphanage. At an early age I became engrossed in Spurgeonic literature, probably because I had to sleep 'in the spare room', a room in my parents' home that had Spurgeon's portrait on the wall and his books on shelves around the room.

The biographies of C H Spurgeon by Carlile and Fullerton first captured my attention, closely followed by the six-volume set by Pike and the four volumes of the *Autobiography*.

As a boy preacher myself, beginning at the age of sixteen among the Baptist Chapels of Hertfordshire, first accompanying my father in his engagements, I longed to be able to say with Spurgeon:

> 'If anybody had said to me, "Somebody has left you twenty thousand pounds", I should not have given a snap of my fingers for it compared with the joy which I felt when I was told that God had saved a soul through my ministry. I felt like a boy who had earned his first guinea, or *like a diver who had been down to the depth of the sea, and brought up a rare pearl*'.

W Y Fullerton commented: 'He was ever seeking such pearls'. When Spurgeon died, his Tabernacle membership stood at 5,000-plus. During the centenary year of his death on 31 January 1892, the year 1992, I gave lectures on Spurgeon in various parts of the country. During my research for such talks I noticed that nobody had collected his 'pearls' into book form for the encouragement of preachers and others.

From the various biographies, his volumes of sermons, and his monthly magazine, *The Sword and the Trowel*, it is possible to make a very precious string of 'pearls'. But I have not collected them just for the reader's enjoyment. Like Spurgeon, I am eager that all Christians should become soul-winners. He himself published a little book called *The Soul Winner*, to encourage his students at his Pastors' College in 'that most royal employment - soul-winning'. It was also meant as a handbook on soul-winning for Sunday school teachers, open-air preachers and other Christian workers.

One of Spurgeon's sermons that greatly impressed me as a young Christian was entitled Soul Winning. It was based upon a text from the Book of Proverbs, and I was intrigued to discover that it could be read forwards or back-to-front, both ways making sense:

'He that winneth souls is wise
He that is wise winneth souls' (Proverbs 11:30).

'Go for souls' was the watchword of General William Booth of the Salvation Army. Spurgeon's

American friend, the evangelist D L Moody, used to pray daily that he might win souls. His prayer has been put into verse:

Lead me to some soul today,
Oh, teach me, Lord, just what to say!
Friends of mine are lost in sin,
And cannot find their way.
Few there are who seem to care,
And few there are who pray;
Melt my heart and fill my life
To win some soul today.

When speaking at the funeral of his ministerial friend, James Smith of Cheltenham, Spurgeon said, 'his was a converting ministry'. Like Booth and Spurgeon he 'went for souls'. These men expected souls to be saved each time they preached.

In this collection of conversion stories, Spurgeon's 'pearls', I have added a Scripture text beneath the title and a prayer, taken from one of Spurgeon's collected prayers, at the conclusion. This has been done so that the reader might use the book for daily devotional reading, not just as a thrilling document describing how Spurgeon was mightily used as a soul-winner.

I have not seen fit to give the source of each account of a conversion. This book is not a thesis for a university doctorate. It is meant to be an encouragement for Christians who long to become soul-winners.

Some of the stories found in various biographies are too short for a chapter on their own. For example,

Spurgeon's first 'pearl' was 'a labourer's wife'. That is all that we know. We do not even know if she was present and saved the first time he ever preached, in the Teversham cottage in Cambridgeshire. All we know is that 'he prized that soul more than all the multitude that came after'. I have therefore collected conversion stories that contain rather more detail. We must not, however, in any way denigrate or 'despise the day of small things'.

Perhaps the greatest 'pearl' of them all was Spurgeon's own conversion; without that there would have been no others to record. I have thus included his own conversion account, told in his own words when preaching on the text that God used for his eternal salvation.

For the sake of those who know little about the great Victorian Baptist preacher, I have added a few biographical notes at the end of the book, also his famous sermon from *The Metropolitan Tabernacle Pulpit* series entitled *Soul Winning*.

1

PAT AND THE PRIEST

'In Him we have redemption through his blood, the forgiveness of sins, in accordance with the riches of God's grace that he lavished on us with all wisdom and understanding' (Ephesians 1:7, 8).

In his early days in London an Irishman came to see Spurgeon in his vestry. Giving the preacher a low bow and calling him 'Yer Riverence' (which Spurgeon at once said was unacceptable!), Pat said that he had been to his priest with a question but had been given an answer which he did not like.

His question was: 'If God is just, He must punish sin, and I deserve to be punished. Yet, God is merciful, and will forgive sins. He has no right to do that. He ought to be just, and punish those who deserve it. How can God be both just and merciful?' Spurgeon replied: 'Through the blood of Christ'.

Pat replied that his priest had given him the

same answer, but had also given him a 'good deal besides that I did not understand'. He wanted to know if it was the blood of Jesus Christ that enabled God to be both just and merciful.

Spurgeon explained the plan of salvation to Pat in these words:

'Now, Pat, suppose you had been killing a man, and the judge had said, "That Irishman must be hanged", you would say, "I should deserve to be hanged". But, Pat, suppose I was very fond of you, can you see any way by which I could save you from being hanged?" "No, sir, I cannot", you would say. "Then, suppose I went to the Queen, and said, 'Please your Majesty, I am very fond of this Irishman; I think the judge was quite right in saying he must be hanged; but let me be hanged instead, and you will then carry out the law'. Now, the Queen could not agree to my proposal; but suppose she could - and God can, for He has power greater than all kings and queens - and suppose the Queen should have me hanged instead of you, do you think the policeman would take you up afterwards?" Pat replied, "No, I should think not; they would not meddle with me; but if they did, I should say, 'What are you doing? Did not that gintleman condescind to be hung for me? Let me alone; shure, you don't want to hang two people for the same thing, do ye?'

Spurgeon replied to Pat, 'Ah, my friend, you have hit it; that is the way whereby we are saved! God must punish sin. Christ said, "My Father, punish me instead of the sinner"; and His Father did. God laid on His beloved Son, Jesus Christ, the whole burden of our sins, and all their punishment and chastisement; and now that Christ is punished for us, God would not be just if He were to punish any sinner who believes on the Lord Jesus Christ. If thou believest in Jesus Christ, the well-beloved and only-begotten Son of God, thou art saved, and thou mayest go on thy way rejoicing. 'Faith,' said Pat, clapping his hands, 'that's the gospel. Pat is safe now; with all his sins about him, he'll trust in the Man that died for him, and so he shall be saved'.

Prayer

O Lord Jesus, our souls fly to Thee. Thou art the only refuge of our heart. Our confidence is fixed upon Thy blood and righteousness, and we believe that these will never fail us. Oh for grace today to take a bleeding Saviour at His word, and to believe Him to be the propitiation for our sins.

2

GIN & TONIC

*'Whoever drinks the water I give him will
never thirst. Indeed, the water I give him will
become in him a spring of water welling up
to eternal life' (John 4:14).*

The London into which Spurgeon came when he
answered the call to become the pastor of New
Park Street Chapel, Southwark, was extremely
depressing. One historian has described it in these
words:

'Contemporary newspapers... [cannot] give an
adequate vision of the abominations that... prevailed in all the working-class quarters - two-thirds
of the whole child population growing up not only
practically without schooling or religious influ-
ences of any kind, but also indescribably brutal
and immoral. ...The flaring *gin-palaces* alone
relieved the monotony of the mean streets and
dark alleys to which they were doomed; graduat-
ing almost inevitably into vice and crime.'

From such grim surroundings, soon after Spurgeon began his ministry in London, a man entered the equally grim-looking chapel building in which Spurgeon (aged 19) was ministering to the eager crowds who flocked to hear him. The grim exterior gave no indication of the fashionable and wealthy congregation who had called Spurgeon to be their leader. By now, however, he was also reaching the more humble folk of that area. At first his large blue-spotted handkerchief offended his fashionable congregation, but now he was among a less critical and more warm-hearted people.

The man who entered had come straight from the gin-palace - his accustomed Sunday night pastime. He could hardly enter for the crowd around the door but managed to push his way through and mount the gallery stairs. He had arrived late and so had to stand during the sermon.

Spurgeon's quick eye saw the man, but knowing nothing about him, began to describe him. 'A word of knowledge' was an unknown phrase in those days, since there were no Charismatics to bandy it about. But as was often the case in Spurgeon's preaching, the Holy Spirit gave him what Spurgeon called 'pulpit inspiration', and he began to speak like this:

'There is a man in the gallery who has come in with no good motive, for he has a gin-bottle in his pocket'. As the preacher went on, the man was startled by the exact description Spurgeon was giving of his character and conduct. He listened attentively to the warnings of the gospel message and the Word of God reached his heart. The grace of God met with him and he was converted there and then. He went home a changed man, walking humbly in the fear of the Lord. The gin-palace had lost a regular customer and eternity had gained a saved sinner.

From having wasted his wages on drink that inflamed his passions and ruined his home life he had tasted of the heavenly tonic, the 'water of life', and he had become a possessor of the riches of heaven which neither moth nor rust can cause to dwindle or destroy.

Prayer:
We would ask now that we may be washed. Bathe us once and for all in the sin-removing fountain. Wash us in the waters of regeneration and give us the renewing of our minds. Oh for daily cleansing. Wash us that we may be clean, O Lord and Master, Thou who didst wash Thy disciples' feet.

3

THE WOULD-BE SUICIDE

*'When a woman who had lived a sinful life in
that town learned that Jesus was eating at the
Pharisee's house, she brought an alabaster
jar of perfume, and as she stood behind him
at his feet weeping, she began to wet his feet
with her tears' (Luke 7:37, 38).*

In 1885 Spurgeon arranged a meeting at his
Haddon Hall Mission for those interested in the
religious, social, and sanitary condition of the
district (i.e. Bermondsey). Among many matters
touched on were those of drink, profanity and
immorality[1].

Immorality took the form of mistresses for the
upper classes and visits to the brothel for the
poorer classes. One young woman employed in a
brothel became so disillusioned with her way of
life that she determined to end it all one Sunday
morning.

---

[1]For a fuller picture of Spurgeon's times see A History of
Spurgeon's Tabernacle, Eric W Hayden, (London 1962;
Pasadena, Texas, USA, 1971 & 1992)

She made her way to Blackfriars Bridge intending to throw herself into the river below and so end her life of suffering and shame and degradation. Passing New Park Street Chapel on the way to the bridge she felt a sudden urge to go inside, thinking she might hear something to her advantage that would stand her in good stead when she later met her Maker.

Owing to the crowded congregation she had to elbow her way up an aisle. She soon realised that she could not retreat. There was no way out again as the crowd had closed ranks behind her.

Spurgeon gave out as his text, 'Seest thou this woman?'. He began by describing the woman in the city who was a notorious public sinner, and then pictured her washing the Saviour's feet with her tears and drying them with the hair of her head. He described how much she loved the Saviour because He had forgiven her so much.

While Spurgeon was preaching the harlot in the aisle was being melted to tears, thinking of her own immoral lifestyle and believing that the whole congregation were seeing her life depicted and not the woman in the gospel story. She repented of her sinful way of life and trusted the Saviour who died for her.

Spurgeon commented that it was his great joy, first of all to be the means of her salvation from death by suicide and then to be the instrument of saving her soul from everlasting condemnation. He stated that many like her, who came first out of curiosity, or to scoff, stayed and remained to pray. They subsequently became disciples of Christ and loyal and warm-hearted members of the church.

Prayer:

We confess that we are by nature lost and by practice ruined. We are altogether as an unclean thing, and all our righteousnesses are as filthy rags. We would look at those dear pierced feet bleeding at heart because of sin, wounded, mangled, crushed by the fall and by our own transgression. Dear Saviour, we do take Thee to be everything to us, our sin-bearer and our sin-destroyer.

4

THE FLAT-MATE

*'Man is destined to die once, and after that to
face judgment' (Hebrews 9:27).*

*'The Lord is coming with thousands upon
thousands of his holy ones to judge everyone,
and to convict all the ungodly of all the ungodly acts they have done in the ungodly way,
and of all the harsh words ungodly sinners
have spoken against him' (Jude 14, 15).*

When Spurgeon was called to be pastor of the
small, thatched-roof chapel at Waterbeach, Cambridgeshire, he knew he was going to a place
notorious for its drunkenness and profanity. One
biographer said that 'it was by no means possible
to describe Waterbeach as a Garden of Eden'.
Spurgeon himself described it as a village in
which 'you see poor wretched beings that once
were men standing or rather leaning against the
posts of the ale-houses or staggering along the
street... [with] houses of the people as dens of
iniquity at which your soul stood aghast'.

The boy preacher was not given a manse to live in but was placed in lodgings. For a time he shared a room with another young man. Noticing that he jumped into bed without praying Spurgeon chided him by asking if he had thought what it would be like, going to sleep prayerless and never again waking. The young man got up again and the two of them talked for two hours until Spurgeon's companion was converted. They both knelt by the bed together while the young man gave his life to Christ.

In the same room, with the same companion, Spurgeon had a vivid vision some nights later. God gave him a sight of the future judgment day. He could not sleep and the next day the congregation at Waterbeach heard such a sermon on the fate of the lost that their faces were white and their knees literally trembled. For many years afterwards, that terrible sermon was recalled by those who had heard it. How many 'pearls' there were as a result we have no means of knowing. Only eternity will reveal it. But it all began with an ungodly flat-mate being challenged about the state of his immortal soul and the reality of judgment and condemnation.

No wonder it was at Waterbeach that he wrote a remarkable hymn. The occasion was the Jubilee Services at Waterbeach Baptist Chapel and it is considered one of the best hymns he ever wrote, and he was only 19 years old at the time. One verse probably has in mind the flat-mate's conversion and his subsequent sermon on judgment:

> When hell, enraged, lifts up her roar,
> When Satan stops my path before,
> When fiends rejoice and wait my end,
> When legion'd hosts their arrows send,
>   Fear not, my soul, but hurl at hell
>   Thy battle-cry, Immanuel.

Prayer:

May we be consciously passed over by the Spirit of condemnation; may we know in our hearts that 'there is therefore now no condemnation to them that are in Christ Jesus'. May we feel the peace-giving power of the Divine absolution. May we come into Thy holy presence with our feet washed in the brazen laver, hearing our great High Priest say to us, 'Ye are clean every whit'.

5

THE TWO BROTHERS

*'I (Hannah) prayed for this child, and the
Lord has granted me what I asked of him'
(1 Samuel 1:27).*

A great many conversions in the early days of
Spurgeon's ministry were a result of his being
vilified in the press or because the man in the street
scoffed or jeered at him. People went to hear him
just because they heard slanderous remarks made
about him.

On one occasion two brothers went to hear the
'odd preacher down the road'. Their mother was
a widow and both of them, while being excellent
in their behaviour while still children, had become
wayward in their youth. They were headstrong
and completely out of control by the mother.
Being a praying mother she took the matter to the
Lord and one Sunday stayed at home instead of
going to church in order to spend the evening in
prayer for her two sons.

Just as she had shut her bedroom door for a time

21

of secret prayer, the elder son called out that he was going 'to hear the minister that preaches down Southwark way; I am told he is an odd man, and I want to hear him preach'. The mother did not think much of C H Spurgeon either, but she was glad her son was going within sound of the Word of God. 'My brother is going with me,' called out the elder son, and so the two of them went to New Park Chapel to hear Spurgeon.

They were both converted that night under the preaching of 'the odd minister' and returned home to break the news to their praying mother. When she opened the door to them, the elder son fell on her neck, crying as if his heart would break, declaring: 'Mother, I have found the Saviour; I am a believer in the Lord Jesus Christ'. She looked at him for a moment and then said, 'I knew it, my son; tonight I have had power in prayer, and I felt that I had prevailed'. 'But,' said the younger brother, 'oh, Mother! I, too, have been cut to the heart, and I also have given myself to the Lord Jesus Christ.'

Some short while afterwards the mother went to see Spurgeon and said, 'You have been the means of the conversion of my two sons; I have never thought of baptism before, but I see it now to be the Lord's own ordinance, so I will be baptised with my children.' Thus for Spurgeon it

was a great joy to lead all three of them down into
the water and baptise them in the Name of the
Father, the Son, and the Holy Spirit. And all this
because one wayward son heard a preacher scorned
by the spiritually indifferent or the religiously
jealous. One common form of reference to Spurgeon in those days was the remark by a ministerial
brother who was envious of the young man's
success: 'the sauciest dog who ever barked in a
pulpit' was the way he referred to him.

Thus did God use strange dress, demeanour
and defamatory remarks to enhance Spurgeon's
reputation as a preacher and to bring under the
sound of the gospel the unsaved that they might be
gloriously converted and become some of Spurgeon's 'pearls'.

Prayer:

Lord, Thou hast heard our prayers, even
when we have hardly thought they could be
answered. We have been unbelieving, but
Thou hast been faithful. We have been
undeserving, but Thy grace has never failed.
Thou hast always been our Helper, ever the
eternal Fountain of good things to Thy
waiting peoples.

6

SAVED BY A BIRTHDAY

*'Jesus declared, I tell you the truth, no-one
can see the kingdom of God unless he is born
again. You should not be surprised at my
saying, You must be born again' (John 3:3, 7).*

When Spurgeon attained his twenty-first birthday
he had a 'pearl' given him as perhaps his choicest
birthday present. He did not know of this welcome
present until some time later.

The night before his birthday he had preached
from the text, 'What is your life?' (James 4:14).
The title was Pictures of Life and Birthday Reflec-
tions. It was also published in a volume entitled
The Pulpit Library, published by James Paul,
containing ten of Spurgeon's sermons before he
began publishing his own annual volumes.

Some weeks later he was visited by a man on
business at the Tabernacle. He told Spurgeon that
he had not only heard the pre-twenty-one sermon
but it had been the means of his salvation.

The man was very depressed at the time and

had contemplated suicide. The sermon encouraged him to go on 'in the battle of life' and he had never descended into the depths of depression again. He then told Spurgeon: 'Though I live a long way from here, no one loves you more than I do, for you were the means of bringing me up out of the horrible pit, and out of the miry clay'. The two men shook hands and Spurgeon rejoiced with him that one of his early sermons had been so used by God the Holy Spirit.

Which part of the 'birthday sermon' appealed to the depressed man? Could it have been the opening sentence?

'It well behoves me, now that another year of my existence has almost gone, standing on the threshold of a fresh era, to consider what I am, where I am going, what I am doing, whom I am serving, and what shall be my reward'.

Or could it have been the closing peroration?

'Such is life! Then make the best use of it, my friends, because it is fleeting. Look for another life, because this life is not a very desirable one, it is so changeable. Trust your life in God's hand because you cannot control its movements; rest in his arms, and rely on his might; for he is able to do for you exceeding abundantly above all that you ask or think; and unto his name be glory for ever and ever.'

Perhaps it was the telling middle section where Spurgeon is expounding life as a pilgrimage:

> 'A pilgrim sets out in the morning, and he has to journey many a day before he gets to the shrine which he seeks. ...sometimes he will be on the mountains, anon he will descend into the valleys... anon he will find himself in the arid desert, where no life is found, and no sound is heard. ...at one time he walks between the rocks, in some narrow gorge, where all is darkness.'

For one whose life was dry, depressing and darkness, Spurgeon's 'pearl' found new life in Christ through being born again of the Spirit. Like Spurgeon he found that he had two birthdays - his natural day of birth and his supernatural experience of being born again.

Prayer:

Oh, for newness of life! Hast Thou not said, 'Behold I make all things new'? Lord, let everything be new in us, and everything living, vividly living, quickened into fullness of life, life more abundantly. Lord, give us to know the power of Thy resurrection.

7

THE CONDEMNED MURDERER

*'If you suffer, it should not be as a murderer
or thief or any other kind of criminal, or even
as a meddler' (1 Peter 4:15).*

Spurgeon's 'pearls' were not only the result of the spoken word, his sermons at the time of delivery. Many began to be converted as a result of the written word, once he began issuing his sermons in a weekly penny series and then as annual bound volumes. One biographer refers to the conversions resulting from the sermons being read as 'miracles of mercy' occurring through the years that followed the publication of the sermons.

On 8 June 1856 Spurgeon preached in the Exeter Hall, London, from Hebrews 7:25: 'Wherefore he is able also to save them to the uttermost that come unto God by him, seeing he ever liveth to make intercession for them'. The sermon was published under the title 'Salvation to the uttermost'. Thirty years later Spurgeon heard how a convicted murderer in South America had been brought to the Saviour through reading it.

This 'pearl' was an Englishman who had committed murder while blind drunk. He was sentenced to life imprisonment but when visited by a Tabernacle member who was on a business trip to Para, Brazil, was found to be healed of his blood-guiltiness and enjoying the bliss of God's pardon.

In prison the man had received a parcel of books from England. Among them was a volume of Spurgeon's sermons. In one sermon Spurgeon mentioned a man who had committed several murders in England and was in Stafford Gaol under sentence of death. The preacher emphasised that even such a man, if he repented, could know God's pardon and peace.

The prisoner in Brazil said to himself, 'If Palmer could be forgiven then so can I.' He then turned to God in repentance and trust and received Christ as his Saviour and Lord. He said, 'I sought the Saviour, and, blessed be God, I found him; and now I am pardoned, I am free; I am a sinner saved by grace.'

'I'm no murderer,' people say when they hear the sin of murder mentioned from the pulpit. What about when we say, or think, 'I wish you were dead'? It is possible to commit murder in the mind as it is to commit adultery in the heart. In that same sermon Spurgeon affirmed that it is possible to be 'Sabbath-breakers' while sitting in church (through wandering thoughts, formality, coldness of heart, and so forth) as it is by going to an amusement park and breaking it there.

The 'Prince of Preachers' (as he was by then referred to) ended his sermon by stating publicly: 'I am no orator, I have no eloquence' but proceeded to rely on the Spirit to do His own work of salvation. 'Spirit of God, make them come! Compel them to come to Christ by sweet constraint, and let not our words be in vain'. His words were not in vain, either when preaching in the Tabernacle or through the printed sermons entitled *The Metropolitan Tabernacle Pulpit* or *The New Park Street Pulpit*.

Prayer:

There is a natural tendency in us towards that which is evil; and even in the hearts of those who are regenerate, that tendency still struggles for the mastery. 'Oh wretched man that I am.' O Lord, we have broken all Thy commandments. We are all condemned by that perfect law; and if sentence were executed upon us, it would only be great justice. Thanks be to Thy holy Name; many of us have fled to Christ, and Thou hast blotted out our sin. We praise Thee for full remission, freely and graciously given, never to be reversed.

8

A PICTURE FOR A PEARL

*'A word aptly spoken is like apples of gold in
settings (pictures) of silver' (Proverbs 25:11).*

On one occasion Spurgeon received a long letter
from a 'pearl' who lived in Norwich. The man had
been a leading light in the 'infidel society' of that
city.

From another infidel this man, a shop-keeper,
bought a pamphlet entitled *Who is this Spurgeon?*
(price 3d). The pamphlet also contained a portrait
of the preacher. The pamphlet and the portrait
were both in the style of a caricature. However, the
man placed the portrait in his shop window,
hoping it would attract passers-by, and improve
business. Not being a bookseller or paper and
magazine shop, the portrait stood out in a conspicuous manner. 'But,' he wrote to Spurgeon, 'I
have taken it down now, for *I am taken down too.*'

It appears he had bought a sermon by Spurgeon
and in it read these words: 'They go on; that step
is safe - they take it; the next is apparently safe -

they take that; their foot hangs over a gulf of darkness'. The word 'darkness' spoke to his heart. He realised he was living in darkness himself. He said to himself, 'True, the way has been safe so far, but I am lost in bewilderment; I cannot go on as I have been going. No, no, no; I will not risk it'. He left home with three words ringing in his ears: 'Who can tell?' He determined not to let another Sunday pass without visiting a place of worship. He felt it would be cowardly of him not to give himself a chance of eternal salvation. Knowing that his infidel friends and associates would laugh, scoff and deride, perhaps call him a turncoat, he nevertheless went to chapel.

At the door of the chapel, he was greeted by the door steward with the words, 'It is Mr So-and-so, isn't it?' So he was well-known and could not hide the fact that he was there.

Sitting waiting for the service to begin, he felt 'fit to burst with anguish'. 'If it be the house of God,' he said to himself, 'may heaven grant me an audience, and I will make a full surrender.' He asked that God would give him a token by which he might know that God existed, and that He would not cast out such a vile offender who had dared to seek His face and pardoning mercy.

Opening the hymn book at random, the first words to catch his eye were:

Dark, dark indeed the grave would be
Had we no light, O God, from Thee!

After mentioning in his letter to Spurgeon how he now knew that he was truly saved, he besought Spurgeon to appeal in his sermons to similar poor wretches like himself 'whose pride has made him in league with hell'. He continued: 'Tell it to the hesitating and the timid; tell it to the desponding Christian, that God is a very present help to all that are in need'.

Another letter followed in which he told Spurgeon how he had gone to the market-place in Norwich and there made a public recantation of his errors and a profession of his faith in Christ. He then burned all his infidel books in the sight of all the people who had gathered around.

Some time later Spurgeon and the man influenced by Spurgeon's portrait met. Together they praised God and magnified Him for His marvellous mercy.

Prayer:
Lord, we thank Thee for Thy long-suffering mercy. Thou hast not cut us down as cumberers of the ground. Thy mercy is not put away from Thy people. Thy mercy flows to us like a river.

9

A MUSIC HALL PEARL

'Then Nathan said to David, You are the man!'
(2 Samuel 12:7).

While Spurgeon's Tabernacle was being built he preached for a time in the Surrey Gardens Music Hall. All classes of people flocked to such an unusual place for a religious service. The Prime Minister was sometimes seen in the congregation, and one biographer describes how 'at no time have so many of the aristocracy made acquaintance with nonconformist worship'. Statesmen, noblemen, distinguished travellers, and many divines came to hear Spurgeon in the Music Hall. Proof that many of them were unused to a religious service was seen by the number who sat reading the newspaper before the service began!

'Looking unto Jesus' was perhaps the most famous and greatly used sermon. It was often mentioned by converts who were brought to Christ hearing it. But it was not only the sermon itself that convicted. Again and again, Spurgeon was given what today would be termed 'a word of knowledge'. One Sunday, for instance, he tells us he deliberately pointed at a man in the vast crowd and said: 'There is a man sitting here, who is a shoemaker; he keeps his shop open on Sundays and it was open last Sabbath morning. He took ninepence, and there was fourpence profit in it. He sold his soul to Satan for fourpence!'

A city missionary, going his rounds, met this man and discovered him reading one of Spurgeon's printed sermons. 'Do you know Mr Spurgeon?' asked the missioner. 'Yes,' replied the man. 'I have every reason to know him; I have been to hear him, and, under his preaching, by God's grace I have become a new creature in Christ Jesus.' He then told the city missionary how he went to the Music Hall and how, sitting in the middle of a long row of seats, Spurgeon looked at him, pointed to him, and told the congregation that he was a shoemaker and kept his shop open on Sundays. He said he would not have minded that but the preacher went on to tell everybody how he had made but fourpence profit that Sunday morning.

Realising it was God speaking to him rather than the preacher he shut up shop the next Sunday. Being afraid to go and hear Spurgeon the next week, in case he should tell the congregation more about him, he left it for a week or two before going again. When he did go the Lord met with him and saved his soul.

Spurgeon often testified to the fact that there were literally dozens of similar cases. He pointed at somebody in the hall without having the slightest knowledge of them, or that what he said about them was correct. Yet he believed the Holy Spirit moved him to point out a particular person and say what he did about them. People went away from the Music Hall and said to their friends and acquaintances: 'Come, see a man that told me all things that ever I did; beyond a doubt, he must have been sent of God to my soul, or else he could not have described me so exactly'. Indeed, some people nudged their neighbour in the row because they had been hard hit.

Prayer:

O Eternal Spirit, with reverence do we worship Thee; for it is by Thee that we come to Jesus, and it is through Jesus that we come to the Father. Oh, Thy wondrous love indwelling in us! We are often astonished as we think of the indwelling of the Holy Spirit: we put it side by side with the incarnation of the ever-blessed Son. O blessed Spirit, make us deeply grateful for both, and because we know the one through the other may we rejoice in each as Thou shalt help us.

10

A PEARL IN A PALACE

'He who has ears, let him hear'
(Matthew 11:15).

The largest congregation Spurgeon ever spoke to in a building was on Wednesday 7 October 1857. There were 23,654 present in the Crystal Palace. It was a 'fast-day service', the occasion being a day of national fasting and prayer to Almighty God, imploring him to assist our nation endeavouring to restore peace and tranquillity in India.

The collection amounted to £500 to which the Crystal Palace Company added £500. Spurgeon gave his services freely, declining to accept any fee for preaching. The service was so exhausting that when he went to bed on the Wednesday night he did not wake again until Friday morning! His wife looked in on him at intervals throughout Thursday but he was sleeping like a baby.

The service was greatly blessed and Spurgeon commented that 'eternity alone will reveal the full results' of that service in the Crystal Palace.

The extraordinary thing is that the one 'pearl' we do know about was a conversion that took place two days before the service was held. This 'set God's seal upon the effort' before the day of the great service arrived.

The preacher was visiting the Crystal Palace to see where they were going to erect his pulpit. In order to test the acoustics of the building Spurgeon stood up and said in a loud voice, 'Behold the Lamb of God, which taketh away the sin of the world'. In one of the galleries, a workman, who knew nothing of what was being done, heard the words, and they came like a heavenly message to his soul. He was smitten with conviction on account of his sinful way of life. Putting down his tools he went home and a spiritual struggle began. It ended when he yielded to Christ and found life and peace by believing in the Lamb of God. It was many years later that the story came out. The man told it to one who was visiting him on his death-bed.

We can only marvel that in days before amplification systems, public address systems, such as we know today, that a man like Spurgeon with a voice 'like a silver bell' could be heard so clearly in such a large building. There must have been much noise from the workmen getting platform and pulpit ready, and other jobs too. But God wanted one man to hear his inspired word, and hearing, believe.

Spurgeon could have said, 'Mary had a little lamb...' as some do today when trying out a microphone. But God's Lamb was more to the point. He could have repeated a succession of numbers - One, two, three... testing, testing. Spurgeon, like Bunyan before him, was bibline - 'prick him anywhere and he bleeds the Bible' it was said of them. So God's word did its own work. Thirteen simple words that contain such a wealth of theology and gospel resulted in a 'pearl' in a crystal palace.

Prayer:

Lord God, we see in Thy crucified Son a sacrifice for sin; we see how Thou hast made Him to be sin for us that we might be made the righteousness of God in Him; and we do over again accept Him to be everything to us. This is the victim by whose blood the covenant is made through faith; this is that Paschal Lamb by the sprinkling of whose blood all Israel is secured; for Thou hast said, 'When I see the blood I will pass over you'.

11

THE DOWN-UNDER SWAGMAN

*'There was a rich man who was dressed in purple
and fine linen and lived in luxury every day. At his
gate was laid a beggar named Lazarus, covered
with sores and longing to eat what fell from the rich
man's table' (Luke 16:19-21).*

One wealthy benefactor paid for Spurgeon's sermons to be printed in *The Australasian* as
advertisements. They were read 'down under' in
homes, public houses and many public places.

The owner of the newspaper was not favour-
ably inclined to carrying such blatantly religious
'copy', especially as his was a sporting paper.
Whereas he might have given special rates for
something religious, he demanded full price for
Spurgeon's sermons, even though the person pay-
ing for them asked several times for a reduction.

The editor asked for the opinion of readers and
was astounded to receive over 400 replies of
appreciation. The benefactor sent these on to
Spurgeon who noted that they came from all parts

of Australia and New Zealand.

One letter came from a 'swagman'[1] who had been travelling about for more than five years looking for a job. Entering a public house he picked up a newspaper lying on the bar and his eye caught the text of one of Spurgeon's sermons: 'Turn, O backsliding children, saith the Lord; for I am married unto you'. He read it right through and realised that it was meeting his deepest need. It showed him his lost condition as a sinner 'of the deepest dye', and yet also encouraged him to look to God for mercy, pardon and peace. He found these at the foot of the cross.

On leaving the public house he determined he would not frequent them again 'unless compelled by circumstances to do so'. At once he began reading the Bible daily and attended church whenever he could. Brought up in the Church of England, he had not darkened the door of any church during the seven years he had been in Australia.

He managed to get a job and each week his employer lent him his copy of *The Australasian* that he might read another sermon by Spurgeon.

---

[1] 'Swagman' - an Australian term for a man who carries his belongings in a 'swag' or bundle. We would call him a tramp or vagrant. The word has been immortalised in the Australian National Anthem - 'Waltzing Matilda' ('Once a jolly swagman...').

When Spurgeon's *Autobiography* was compiled by Mrs Spurgeon and his private secretary, the name of the benefactor was still unknown. He merely signed himself when writing to Spurgeon: 'I am, Yours truly, ****'. What a day of reunion and rejoicing it will be when benefactor, swagman and preacher all meet in heaven!

Prayer:

O God our Father, we do remember well when we were called to Thee; with many sweet and wooing voices we were bidden to return. Thou didst Thyself hang out the lights of mercy that we might know the way home, and Thy dear Son Himself came down to seek us. We come again now to the cross whereon the Saviour bled; we give another look of faith to Him. We do avow ourselves today to be the Lord's.

12

SAVED AT SEA

*'(They) went out on the sea in ships; they
were merchants on the mighty waters. They
saw the works of the Lord, his wonderful
deeds in the deep' (Psalm 107: 24, 25).*

Victorian British workmen looked upon Spurgeon as 'one of them'. Besides maintaining a
30-year ministry at the Metropolitan Tabernacle
on Sundays, Mondays and Thursdays, he edited a
monthly magazine, revised his sermons for publication, and had the oversight of the institutions
connected with the Tabernacle. Besides all that he
found time to preach throughout the British Isles
and also on the Continent. He paid his first visit to
Ireland in August 1858, preaching in Belfast. He
visited Ireland many times after that but what
thrilled his heart as much as preaching to the
crowded congregations on the Emerald Isle was to
cross on the ferry from Holyhead to Dublin, rough
passages as some of them were.

Believing that 'rough sailors' were difficult to
reach with the gospel he was pleasantly surprised

to find they were 'queuing up' to shake his hand as he boarded the ship. He wondered how they knew of him, especially when some began calling him 'Brother'! Usually Irish sailors would have greeted a minister of the gospel as 'Father', so why 'Brother'?

On one occasion he found that all the crew except for three men were Christians. They had experienced a 'sudden visitation of the Spirit of God' on board ship.

They were not all Irishmen. One took out a Welsh edition of Spurgeon's sermons with Spurgeon's portrait on the cover. It was a leather-covered book but dog-eared and worn. Sometimes during a smooth passage he would gather people around him and read passages from a sermon (presumably translating from Welsh into English), and then they would sing a hymn. One passenger stood laughing during a hymn so one of the Christian crew prayed for him aloud. The man was struck down under Holy Spirit conviction and on disembarking knelt on the quayside and begged God to show mercy to him and pardon his sins.

Most of the crew had been 'visited' in the same way and had become 'joyful and happy men, serving the Lord'. They organised a morning prayer meeting before the ship set sail and another when she docked. One who had been present at one of these prayer meetings said to Spurgeon, 'I should like you to hear the men pray; I never heard such pleading before, they pray as only sailors can pray'.

Travelling another time on a different steamer, Spurgeon discovered exactly the same conditions. He walked among the crew, talking to them, discovering that those who had been 'loudest with their oaths, are now loudest with their songs; those who were the most daring sons of Satan, have become the most earnest advocates of the truth'.

Having heard such a ship's crew he reached the conclusion that 'of all men who can preach well, seamen are the best' and that 'the hardy British tar has got a heart that is not made of such cold stuff as many of the hearts of landsmen; and when that heart is once touched, it gives big beats, and sends great pulses of energy right through his whole frame; and with his zeal and energy, what may he not do, God helping him, and blessing him?'

Prayer:
Come Lord, with a live coal from off the altar, and set Thy churches on a blaze again. Oh for the days of the Son of Man, times of refreshing! We would see millions converted to God. We would see the whole Church quickened to the fullest extent by the indwelling Spirit. Thou canst do it Lord. Do it for Thy name and glory's sake.

13

THE SAVING OF SATAN

'The coming of the lawless one will be in accordance with the work of Satan displayed in all kinds of counterfeit miracles, signs and wonders, and in every sort of evil that deceives those who are perishing. They perish because they refused to love the truth and so be saved'
(2 Thessalonians 2:9, 10).

During Spurgeon's pastoral 'silver wedding' (25 years at the Tabernacle) he mentioned the fact in a sermon that there had been nine thousand people joining the church during that period. Many more, of course, had been converted through his preaching and writing, without becoming members of the Tabernacle.

He stressed the fact that not all had been saved following conviction of sin through hearing of 'the terrors of the law'. Over fifty per cent were won for Christ 'by gentler means', through seeing Christ's lovely character and substitutionary death for instance. 'Satan', as he was nicknamed, did experience the terrors of the law. Like the apostle

Paul he called himself 'the chief of sinners'. His nickname was given him in the village where he lived because of his blatant deprived life.

'Satan' became a sailor. Another seaman had been instrumental in leading the rest of the ship's crew to the Lord and gave himself one more chance to sail with 'Satan' and plead with him. He failed, but back on shore invited him to the Tabernacle to hear Spurgeon.

The one thing in Spurgeon's favour was that he was brought up very near to the Essex village where this man lived. It was a Sunday morning service and Spurgeon preached on 'soul-murder'. The Holy Spirit applied the Word of God to 'Satan's' heart and he sat and sobbed and sobbed during the sermon until he thought, 'People are noticing me'. He left the Tabernacle a changed man, a new creation in Christ Jesus. Satan had been conquered in more senses than one! He was soon living and walking as an out-and-out Christian, witnessing for the spread of the Kingdom of God.

Spurgeon commented that just as there had been a great variety of converts during his ministry, so the means of their conversion was as varied.

It was not only public preaching that resulted in conversions; he took every opportunity of witness and presenting a challenge. Once he was staying

at a deacon's house when preaching elsewhe.
After tea he walked to the church at which he was
booked to preach and asked the deacon's son who
was showing the way, 'Do you love my Master?'
The young man replied, 'I have walked to this
chapel with ministers for several years, and not
one of them ever asked me such a question before'!

For 'Satan' it was the powerful preaching of
the Word; for a boy brought up in a sheltered home
it was 'a word fitly spoken'. The sovereign God
saves his elect when and how he wills.

Prayer:

Help us to overcome every tendency to evil
which is still within us, and enable us to
wear armour of such proof that the arrows
of (Satan) may not penetrate it, that we may
not be wounded again by sin. Deliver us, we
pray Thee, from doubts within and fears
without, from depression of spirit, and from
the outward assaults of the world.

14

AN OBEDIENT MOTHER

'To the chosen lady and her children, whom I
love in the truth - and not I only, but also all who
know the truth - because of the truth, which lives
in us and will be with us for ever' (2 John 1, 2).

The congregation at the Tabernacle were also
expected to be 'pearl divers' if they were believers. Often Spurgeon would give a short and simple
piece of advice during a sermon, sometimes in the
form of a simple request, and the Lord set his seal
on his words.

Unbelievers were often asked to go home, sit
quietly alone with a pencil and paper. They were
asked to write one of two words on the paper:
Condemned or Forgiven. Several found Christ in
that way; in particular, one young man first wrote,
Condemned, then as he read it began to cry with
a breaking heart. He tore the paper up and put it in
the fire. Taking another piece he wrote, Forgiven,
and soon applied for church membership.

Another man began to write, Condemned, when

his little daughter caught hold of his hand and begged him not to write it. His wife joined in the entreaty and he too changed the word to, Forgiven.

One Sunday evening Spurgeon spoke to all mothers in the congregation and asked them to go home and talk to their daughters about their soul's condition. 'But she will be in bed,' a mother will reply. 'Then wake her up, talk to her and pray with her... then let her fall asleep again.'

There was a mother that night who took Spurgeon's simple advice to heart. She went home and did exactly as he suggested. The girl was delighted and said, 'Oh, mother! I am glad you have spoken to me about Jesus; for months, I have been wishing you would do so.'

It was not long afterwards that the mother took her daughter to see Spurgeon in his vestry because she felt she should join the church.

Many years later, Dr G Campbell Morgan was talking with his four sons, all of whom were preachers. He said to one of them, Howard, 'Which of us do you think is the best preacher?' Looking straight at his father, Howard said, 'Mother!' Spurgeon knew that.

Often mothers have 'pulpits' and a sphere of influence that is denied to fathers. Eternity will reveal the tremendous part mothers have played in the salvation of sons and daughters, and grand-

mothers too with their special relationship to their
grandchildren.

Prayer:

We would pray for our children, that they
might be saved. Some of us can no longer
pray for our children's conversion, our
prayers are heard already. But there are
others who have children who vex them and
grieve their hearts. O God, save sons and
daughters of godly people. Let them not
have to sigh over their children as Eli did
and as Samuel did, and may they see their
sons and daughters become the children of
the living God.

15

A PRODIGAL PEARL

'While he was still a long way off, his father saw him and was filled with compassion for him'
(Luke 15:20).

Difficult doctrines were often the means of salvation as Spurgeon preached them. Some people imagined that because Spurgeon was an avowed Calvinist his doctrinal sermons would be unlikely to save the simple, homely work-people who frequented the Tabernacle. Far from it. He once said, 'I have heard of scores brought to the Saviour by a discourse upon election... God frequently blesses the Word in the very opposite manner to that in which I thought it would be blessed, and He brings very, very many to know their state by nature by doctrines which I should have thought would rather have comforted believers than awakened the unconverted. I am constantly driven back to the great foundation truth of Divine Sovereignty.'

One day an old minister of the gospel was

talking to Spurgeon and suddenly put his hand into his pocket and brought out a tattered letter. It appears he had a son whom he thought would be with him till old age. Instead, after disgracing himself, he ran away from home, saying that he was going to America.

The old minister received a letter from America in which the son asked for forgiveness for the many wrongs he had done and grief he had caused his father. What happened was that on the day he left for America he had time to spare before his ship set sail. He went to Spurgeon's Tabernacle just to see what it was like. In the sermon he heard Spurgeon say: "Perhaps there is a runaway son here. The Lord call him by his grace!" In the letter, the son added, 'And He did call me.'

Spurgeon was given the letter to read for himself. When he had finished it the brother minister said, 'Now my son is dead, and he has gone to heaven; and I love you, and shall continue doing so as long as I live, because you were the means of bringing him to Christ.'

The son had seen himself as the object of God's electing love, and what was a hard and difficult doctrine for some, especially the opponents and critics of Spurgeon, was for him both comforting and strengthening and saving.

On arrival in America the son had found a good

job with prospects, and God had prospered him. He had also found an evangelical church which he joined, and spent the rest of his life in his Redeemer's service.

No wonder Spurgeon commented in the words of the hymn-writer:

God moves in a mysterious way,
His wonders to perform.

And no wonder he staunchly preached and declared and defended the Calvinistic doctrines of total depravity, unconditional election, limited atonement, irresistible grace and the perseverance of the saints.

Prayer:
We pray today that Thy truth may prevail against the many anti-Christs that have gone forth against it. Our Father, restore a pure language to Thy Zion once again. Take away, we pray Thee, the itching for new doctrine, the longing for that which is thought to be scientific and wise above what is written, and may Thy church come to her moorings, may she cast anchor in the truth of God and there abide.

16

THE TWO SISTERS

'I commend to you our sister Phoebe, a servant of the church in Cenchrea. I ask you to receive her in the Lord in a way worthy of the saints and to give her any help she may need from you, for she has been a great help to many people, including me'
(Romans 16:1, 2).

When Spurgeon spoke or wrote about those converted under his ministry, either through his preaching or his writing, he never made out that it was success all along the line. He said that he was always amazed at 'the ingenuity with which they resist the entrance of the truth into their hearts'.

Often he had to go through the simple plan of salvation again and again. He was often astounded at the aptitude of simple people for finding reasons why they should not believe in Jesus Christ. He said that sometimes he felt like a fox-hunter as he tracked the enquirer to his hole and then tried to unearth him. Sometimes there were so many 'ifs', 'buts', 'perhaps' and 'but I don't feel this or that',

that he wondered if they would be saved in the end.

One day a lady 'Phoebe' brought two young sisters to him in the vestry. They had both been under the sound of the gospel for a time and were deeply impressed by it. Their regret was that they were having to move away and would no longer be able to attend the Tabernacle services. He asked them directly, 'Have you believed in the Lord Jesus Christ?'. One said she was 'trying hard to believe'. That would not do for Spurgeon. 'Did you ever tell your father you were trying hard to believe him?' he asked her. He managed to get her to see that would be an insult to her earthly father. He begged her to believe in Jesus who is more worthy of faith than the best of human fathers. Her reply was that she could not realise that she was saved.

Once more he went on to explain the gospel. He said that the Scriptures plainly state that 'God bears testimony to His Son, that whosoever trusts in the Lord Jesus Christ is saved'. She was then asked: 'Will you make him out to be a liar now, or will you believe His Word?' While he spoke she started as if astonished and in a startled voice said, 'Oh, sir, I see it all; I am saved. Do bless Jesus for me; He has shown me the way and He has saved me. I see it all'.

The 'Phoebe' who had brought them to the

vestry knelt down with them, and Spurgeon knelt too, and with full hearts blessed and magnified God for a soul brought into the light. The other young woman remained in darkness. She just could not see the simplicity of the gospel as had her sister. But Spurgeon added when telling of the incident: 'I feel sure she will do so; but it seemed strange that, both hearing the same words, one should come out into clear light, and the other should remain in the gloom'. Perhaps to a Calvinist it should not have been so strange, for one might have been one of the elect and the other unchosen. But then, Spurgeon not only believed in divine sovereignty but in human responsibility!

Prayer:
Lord God the Holy Ghost, may faith grow in men; may they believe in Christ to the saving of their souls. May their little faith brighten into strong faith, and may their strong faith ripen into the full assurance of faith. May we believe God fully.

17

SAVED THROUGH STICKABILITY

'Therefore, my dear brothers, stand firm. Let nothing move you. Always give yourselves fully to the work of the Lord, because you know that your labour in the Lord is not in vain'
(1 Corinthians 15:58).

Tabernacle members would often go 'fishing' on the streets, in pairs, to invite passers-by into the church to hear Spurgeon.

Two such, manual workers, one of whom was an athlete who had won many events and prizes, would each take a side of the street. One Sunday morning one of them gave a tract to a man passing by who then crossed over the road. The second 'fisherman' heard him swear and say in a loud voice, 'What's the use of giving me a tract? I shall be in hell in an hour'.

The two members, 'hunting for souls' as they put it, followed the man until they caught up with him. On questioning him about being in hell within an hour the man said, 'This world is worse than hell and I'll be out of it in an hour'. 'No, you won't,' replied the athlete, 'for I mean to stick by you; and I won't leave you for an hour, go where you may.'

They took him into a coffee-shop and gave him a good breakfast, believing like William Booth, that it is no use trying to preach the gospel to a man with an empty stomach.

Actually the man had had no food for three days, so the two 'soul-doctors' decided to repeat their prescription and invited the man home to share their humble Sunday lunch.

In the afternoon they took him to a Tabernacle Bible class and then to the evening service. While listening to Spurgeon his heart was touched and he was receptive to the gospel message. He was brought to a knowledge of the Saviour.

After the service he told them his story. He had left his wife in the North of England about four or five months previously. He had come to London to 'make his fortune' but had spent the time in poverty, dissipation and sinful ways.

A letter, explaining the man's change of heart was sent to his wife. She, a Wesleyan Methodist, had been praying for him, not daring to believe that God still had a purpose for him separately or both of them together. He returned to her and together they sat at the Lord's Table rejoicing in his new-found salvation and their joyful reunion.

How often there were humble people who were links in the chain before eventually salvation came through the powerful preaching of their Pastor!

Prayer:

Create, we beseech Thee, a soul thirst in such as are self-satisfied. Breed a sharp hunger in the hearts of those who have been content with the good things of time and sense. May they long after something more enduring, more satisfying; and when Thou hast set them longing, reveal Christ Jesus to them, and let them see how He can fill the soul with peace and joy. Do, Father, grant to Thy servants the great privilege and honour of conducting some to the Saviour.

18

A PEARL ON WHEELS

'The Spirit told Philip, Go to that chariot and stay near it. Then Philip ran up to the chariot... so (the eunuch) invited Philip to come up and sit with him... then Philip told him the good news about Jesus' (Acts 8:29, 30, 35).

He was a Victorian 'Steptoe', driving his horse and cart through the streets of London. He was completely irreligious, never attending church himself and certainly not in contact with any churchgoers. No one ever spoke to him about God or Christ.

One day, when crossing London Bridge, a man jumped on the back of his cart. He was just about to lash him off with his whip when the man said he had a message for him. His 'stowaway' clambered from the back of the cart to sit with him up front. 'What's your message, then?' he asked. 'It's a message from God to your soul.' The driver swore at his passenger hoping he would jump off and leave him alone, all to no avail.

'I've a message for you, and you are just the man I was after. I knew you were a swearing man, for that first attracted my attention to you.' The driver replied, 'Well, make it short then.'

The passenger told the driver of the cart that he knew of a Saviour for sinners, for swearers like him, and began to describe the after-life for the unsaved. Then, before he jumped off the cart he made the driver promise to go and hear Spurgeon at the Metropolitan Tabernacle.

Being a man who kept his promises, whatever other faults he had, he got up early the following Sunday morning and made his way to the Tabernacle. The door steward conducted him to a seat and after the service asked him how he had enjoyed it. 'No, I did not; that is not the sort of thing that I care about; I don't believe in religion.' 'Ah, but you will,' replied the Tabernacle member. The potential 'pearl' left for home hoping he would never see him again.

Some weeks later the driver saw the Tabernacle member as he was going down Blackfriars Road. He slipped round the first corner hoping to 'lose' him, but the man ran after him. After asking how he was, the Christian remarked that he believed that one day the driver would become a Christian. He also added that he would never leave him alone until he was a Christian.

As the driver went into his house he had great difficulty in shaking off his tenacious 'friend'. He did not want him in his home, he and his wife were both too fond of drink and they had little furniture, none of it to be proud of. Indeed, it was a quite miserable and squalid place. To get rid of his persistent companion he promised to go to the Tabernacle the next Sunday.

Again he kept his promise and became a Christian. Within six months, he had persuaded four other men to go with him and hear the gospel.

Prayer:

There are strangers within Thy courts: they are unknown to us, but Searcher of all hearts, Thou knowest them. May they hear a sermon they will never forget. May the arrows of God stick so fast that they may never be drawn out, except by that healing Hand that once was pierced.

19

SANITY RESTORED

'When they came to Jesus, they saw the man who had been possessed by the legion of demons, sitting there, dressed and in his right mind' (Mark 5:15).

Spurgeon, like Job and Elijah before him, was subject to bouts of depression. For that reason he was often able to help enquirers who came to him with the same problem. Since 'salvation' in the New Testament means, literally, 'wholeness', it is concerned with our minds and bodies as well as our souls.

Once when he was in the midst of 'a fearful depression of spirit' (as he himself described it), just before he set off for Mentone in the south of France for a rest, he preached on the words, 'My God, my God, why hast Thou forsaken me?'

He was preaching to himself and his own condition as much as to others who were suffering the same way. He said that he was 'as much qualified to preach from that text as ever [he] expected to be'. He also hoped that few of his brethren would suffer as he did. He felt that he was experiencing to the full 'the horror of a soul forsaken by God'.

It is no wonder that after preaching a man came to the vestry seeking an interview. As he entered Spurgeon saw a man who was as 'nearly insane as he could be and yet be out of an asylum'. His eyes started out of his head and he said that he would have utterly despaired if he had not heard such a message as Spurgeon's sermon contained. Wanting more time with him Spurgeon asked him back the following night, Monday, when he usually sat in his vestry for several hours, interviewing candidates for baptism and membership.

They talked in more detail and Spurgeon obviously recommended him to seek what today we would call psychiatric help.

Five years later Spurgeon was preaching from the words, 'The Almighty hath vexed my soul'. After the service the same man came to see him in the vestry. This time he looked 'as different as noonday from midnight, or as life from death'. The preacher told him that he had often thought about him and wondered whether he had been brought into perfect peace. The man replied, 'Yes, you said I was a hopeful patient, and I am sure you will be glad to know that I have walked in the sunlight from that day till now'. Everything was changed and altered with the man. Spurgeon commented that he was glad his own sorrowful feelings had enabled him to sympathise with him and guide him with wise counsel. But how wonderful to be able to say: 'I would go into the deeps a hundred times to cheer a downcast spirit: it is good for me to have been afflicted that I might know how to speak a word in season to one that is weary'.

Prayer:
May our faith grow exceedingly. May we have an experience of Thy goodness, and feel ashamed ever to entertain a doubt, and when a dark thought ever crosses our mind which would make us mistrust, may we chase it away as a strange and vain thought, which must not even lodge, much less dwell, within our hearts.

20

A PEARL BENEATH THE GALLERY

*'He came and preached peace to you who were far
away and peace to those who were near'
(Ephesians 2:17).*

A man living on the south coast was experiencing
business failure and marriage failure. These outward troubles, plus a 'backsliding heart', caused
him to become like Job and 'Curse God and die'.
Believing he was eternally damned he decided to
end his life and go to hell sooner rather than later.
He went down to the sea shore but decided his
body would be washed up where he was well-
known.

His next plan was to go to London where he was
not known and so end his life in the Big City.
Taking a train to town, after telling his wife he was
only going for the weekend, he wandered from
street to street looking for a good place in which
to commit suicide. At every likely spot there were
too many people, who seemed to be watching him.
He found lodging for the night in Kennington

Lane, intending to take his life on Sunday when the wharves would be closed to traffic and a lonely spot could be found.

After breakfast he went out and asked the way to London Bridge. Suddenly he came across a large building with a crowd of people going in. He enquired what was going on and discovered it was Spurgeon's Tabernacle. Hardly knowing what he was doing he joined the queue on the steps and found himself carried in by the crowd pushing forward. He found himself on the landing of the top gallery, and since every seat was taken he stood in what he considered to be a dark recess.

He thought nothing of Spurgeon's prayer and could not join in the Amen. Neither could he join in the singing of the hymns. Then Spurgeon gave out his text: 'Say unto my soul, I am thy salvation'. Coming to the platform rail Spurgeon looked straight at the man and repeated the text: 'Say unto my soul, I am THY salvation'. He began to listen eagerly and God began to speak to him. He stood with eyes fixed on the preacher and his mouth open. Suddenly Spurgeon pointed straight at him and spoke to 'one standing far away in the gallery'. Before the end of the sermon the man's handkerchief was wet with tears, but they were tears of joy. At the close of the service he began to make his way out of the building shouting, 'Let me out or I shall knock somebody down!' 'Are you out of your mind?' someone asked. 'No, thank God! Not out of it, but in it for the first time for many a long day'.

For several hours he wandered the streets, oblivious of everyone and everything, his heart full of joy and praise. From then on, having returned home, he never lost the assurance of his salvation.

Prayer:

Some here once prayed, but they have backslidden, and now they have forgotten their hiding place, their resting place. So long is it since they enjoyed prayer that now this morning they are quite strange to it. Come, Holy Spirit, bring the wanderer back. Dear Shepherd, fetch home the stray sheep, and since it may be too lame to come home, put it on Thy shoulder and bear it home rejoicing. Glorify the power of Thine arm as well as the love of Thine heart in bringing home Thy wanderers.

21

THE SILVERSMITH'S APPRENTICE

*'About that time there arose a great disturbance
about the Way. A silversmith named Demetrius,
who made silver shrines... said... There is danger
that our trade will lose its good name'*
(Acts 19:23, 27).

A father living in a country town apprenticed his
son to a London silversmith. For some time all
went well as the young man applied himself to
learning the craft. One day, however, the father
received a letter saying that the son had robbed his
master. Hurrying up to London the father discovered that it was all too true. His indentures were
cancelled and the son left his situation in disgrace.

As father and son were walking through the
City of London to make their way home the boy
suddenly darted away and disappeared. The police searched for him in vain but the father and
mother lived for years as two heart-broken parents.

One Sunday evening they purposely stayed

away from evening service to spend time quietly reading God's Word and praying for their lost son. They knelt down together and asked that God would stop the boy in his sinful tracks and bring him back to them. Later that evening their servant returned from church and said that she had heard nothing of the preacher's message for she too felt constrained to pray for 'Master Harry'.

That same night some men were passing by the Metropolitan Tabernacle on their way to break into a silversmith's shop and steal as many valuables as they could. One of them suddenly said, 'Harry, nip up those steps and see what the time is'. He ran up the steps, opened the door, looked for the clock, but stood in the aisle. Spurgeon was preaching about the dying thief. To Harry the preacher was pointing directly at him as he said in ringing tones, 'If there is a thief here tonight, Jesus Christ can save him'. The arrow hit its mark. Harry went back to his lodgings to pray, and there on his knees received Christ as Saviour.

A week later there was a knock at the door of the old folk's home in that country town. The father opened it and there before him stood his long-lost son. The Saviour's story of the Prodigal Son was re-enacted: tears, confession, forgiveness, welcome, restoration and joy. Doubtless there was feasting too! But their joy was as nothing when compared with the joy among the angels in heaven over one sinner who repents.

> *Prayer*:
> Our Father, 'forgive us our trespasses as we forgive them that trespass against us'. We do very freely and very heartily and very truly forgive anybody who may have aggrieved us. Do Thou so with Thy children, and let us feel of a certainty now that we are perfectly reconciled with God, and that we are one with Thee, and speak with Thee as a man speaketh with his friend.
> If any of us have wandered and are not aware of it, bring us back at all events; oh, make us like Christ, we do pray Thee, make us like Christ.

22

INFLUENCED BY A DIAMOND

'Judah's sin is engraved with an iron tool, inscribed with a flint (diamond, AV) point, on the tablets of their hearts and on the horns of their altars' (Jeremiah 17:1).

Sinners are convicted by the Holy Spirit in most unusual ways and sometimes in the most unusual of places. It is not always in a church building but the experience frequently drives them towards the House of God afterwards, where conviction is followed by conversion.

In Spurgeon's time a man who had lived for many years 'in the service of sin', living dissolutely and dangerously, desired to sell his house and buy a new one. He visited the estate agent and was given a key to view what seemed to be a 'desirable property'. He declined the offer of the agent to accompany him saying that he preferred to go alone. He went over the ground floor, room by room, then the first floor rooms. There was an attic also, so he went up the stairs to view it. As he went in he saw something scratched on the window pane. Close up he could see that there were words etched with the point of a diamond. He staggered and then began violently trembling. These were the words he read:

PREPARE TO MEET THY GOD

The Spirit of God, the Spirit of conviction, rooted him to the spot as in an agony of soul he cried out, 'Lord, have mercy on me! Lord, save me!' At long last his legs felt strong enough to take him downstairs again and out of the house, but the message, 'Prepare to meet thy God', followed him. He lost all pleasure in his favourite sport - fox-hunting. He tried to put the words out of his thoughts by consorting with evil companions. He became utterly miserable as the words of warning from God's Word dominated his thinking and haunted him wherever he went.

After several weeks had passed, his eye caught a notice that advertised a religious meeting at which Spurgeon was to preach. It was in a village about sixteen miles from where he lived. He said to himself, 'I'll go and hear that man'. He ordered his horse and rode the sixteen miles, hoping to hear something that would bring peace and relief to his troubled mind and conscience.

Spurgeon's text was: 'Come unto Me, all ye that labour and are heavy laden, and I will give you rest'. During the course of his sermon, Spurgeon made an earnest appeal for repentance and faith in Christ. The conscience-stricken sinner became a believer and left the Village Chapel a new man in Christ. Instead of a diamond-etched warning, 'Prepare to meet thy God', dominating his thoughts, he knew that he himself was now engraved upon the hands of God and had a new name written down in glory.

Prayer:

O God, remember any in this house that have never known the griefs of Christ because they have never themselves grieved over sin. O Father, let the Holy Spirit come upon them as the Spirit of bondage, convincing them of sin, of righteousness, and of judgment. And then let Him come as the sweet Spirit of liberty, leading them to the joy and peace in believing which come through the eternal merits and the precious blood of our redeeming Lord.

23

TO THE JEW FIRST

*'Brothers, my heart's desire and prayer to God
for the Israelites is that they may be saved'
(Romans 10:1).*

The story of how three young men came into the
Tabernacle one Sunday and kept their hats on is
well known. They were not Jews, who keep their
heads covered in the synagogue, but Spurgeon put
them in their place by referring to them as Jewish
worshippers. Those who came to scoff, mock, and
ridicule were themselves the object of ridicule.

On the other hand, Spurgeon was very impressed by a Jew's help in winning him a 'pearl'
from the depths of the ocean.

An omnibus passenger one Sunday saw the
crowd waiting to get into the Metropolitan Tabernacle. The man next to him on the bus was a Jew.
The man remarked to the Jew: 'The humbug
always attracts the people'.

The Jew turned to him and asked him if he
would not like to see such a crowd looking into his

shop window and wanting to get inside to make many purchases. He said he had ridden past the Tabernacle for twenty-eight years (most of Spurgeon's ministry there, in fact) and had always seen the crowds waiting to get in.

Turning to his companion, the Jew asked him, 'If your shop had been crowded for twenty-eight years, and anybody said that you did not sell a good article, what would you reply?'

His fellow bus passenger was more than a little discomforted, for he knew that if his goods had not been satisfactory then they would not have continued coming to his shop. 'Now I am a Jew, yet I am inclined to go in and listen to what Mr Spurgeon has to say, because I see these crowds of people going in to hear him.'

We are not told if the Jew did eventually go in, but his fellow passenger on the bus did. He said to himself, 'I have been buying the wrong article. That Jew spoke very sensibly,' and so he went and heard Spurgeon for himself.

He not only visited the shop (the Tabernacle), he examined the article (the truth of the gospel message), and then he made his purchase (but on God's terms - 'without money and without price').

Yes, God uses some very peculiar instruments at times to carry out his purposes and to influence men and women to seek the Saviour. Since He is sovereign He can use whom He will, and when and where.

Prayer:

We would offer a prayer to Thee for those who are quite strange to the work of the Spirit of God, who have never owned their God, who have lived as if there were no God. Open their eyes that they may see God even though that sight should make them tremble and wish to die.

24

A PEARL NECKLACE

*'People will come from east and west and
north and south, and will take their places at
the feast in the kingdom of God'
(Luke 13:29).*

A shepherd was looking after some sheep in Australia. He picked up a sheet of newspaper which the wind had blown over the plains. Glancing at a few sentences he was drawn to read on. Soon he was eagerly reading a sermon by the English preacher, Charles Haddon Spurgeon. If he had known the contents were a sermon before he began reading he would have crumpled the sheet up and thrown it away. Now he carefully preserved it and from time to time read the sermon over and over again. Finally it led him to the cross of Christ for salvation.

A parcel sent from Australia to the wife of a publican in England was wrapped in newspaper which contained a Spurgeon sermon. The woman read it and trusted Christ for salvation.

A young woman went into the vestry to see Spurgeon and asked if it was possible to be saved instantly. 'Yes,' said Spurgeon, and gave her Scriptural proof. 'But,' she replied, 'my grandfather said it took him six months and they nearly put him into a lunatic asylum!' Spurgeon pointed out that distress saves no one. 'I see it,' she cried out, and there and then received Christ into her heart.

A Dutchman from Flushing came into the vestry and told Spurgeon he could not trust Christ. 'Why not? What has He done? What have you got against His character?' 'Nothing,' replied the Dutchman. 'Then, you are commanded by the gospel to believe on the Lord Jesus Christ and be saved.' The Dutchman said, 'Why did I not see it before?' He trusted Jesus for salvation, saying, 'I am well repaid for coming from Flushing.'

On Sunday evening, 10 August 1897, regular congregation members gave up their usual seats so that strangers might occupy them. Spurgeon preached on 'The Plague of the Heart'. In the congregation were workmen in their working clothes, West-end people dressed in the height of fashion, and sober businessmen. Higher and lower ranks were well-represented. The clergy were there in force as were soldiers in their conspicuous red uniforms. It was a great crush and at the close of the service Spurgeon's 'spiritual sharp-shooters gathered up their share of the wounded' - not through being crushed by the crowd present - but 'wounded by the Word'. At a later date others who had been convicted came forward for baptism and membership.

Mr *** was sitting one Sunday as a spectator at the Lord's Table when Spurgeon spoke a few words to the unconverted. The preacher looked straight at him and said, 'You ought not to be there; this is your place, at the table with God's people'. Not long afterwards the old man was baptised in his home chapel and became a member of the church.

Prayer:

Lord, compel men to come near their God. They will have to come to Thee: they will have to come before Thy Judgment Seat; let them not refuse the Mercy Seat. While yet the day of grace lasts, let them not turn their backs on God, but rather may they seek Thee now with full purpose of heart and seek till they find salvation.

25

SUPPOSE I'D DROWNED!

'A furious squall came up, and the waves broke over the boat, so that it was nearly swamped. Jesus was in the stern, sleeping on a cushion. The disciples woke him and said to him, Teacher, don't you care if we drown?' (Mark 4:37, 38).

A well-known sawmill owner in Australia had not been to church for twenty-five years and boasted that during that time he had not met a Christian man. He had lived all his life, as he put it, 'in the darkness of sin'. He did not know the difference between the denominations, and could not care less, believing them all to be grossly in error. He despised everything to do with the church.

One day he lost five of his companions through drowning. This had a salutary effect upon him, especially as he thought, 'What if I had been among their number?' He began to think of the weeping and wailing of the lost souls in hell. To have thought like that he must have had some childhood connection with spiritual things, perhaps through early Sunday school days. At the same time he began to pray to God, although he knew nothing about salvation through faith in Christ.

He lived for the next two years in awful agony, having no spiritual person to guide him and knowing nothing about any preacher who might help him if he went to hear him.

One day, however, a friend paid a visit to Sydney, and on his return gave him a volume of Spurgeon's sermons. He read them eagerly and received, as he put it, 'mighty light and comfort from them'. He came to one with the title, 'Seeking for Jesus'. As he read it God spoke to his heart. He felt that his sins were pardoned and that he could sing out loud for joy. It was about midday one Sunday when this glorious change took place and he remembered the exact spot where it occurred.

When he gave his testimony to a Wesleyan minister in New South Wales (who passed it on to Spurgeon) he said that it had occurred ten years before and for a decade he had been telling the story of the cross wherever he found opportunity.

In the Wesleyan Minister's letter to Spurgeon, reporting the conversion he added a PS: 'At our meeting last night an old gentleman stated that twenty-one years ago he was led to decision through reading a sermon of yours, entitled, Now. He is today a consistent Christian. To God be the praise and glory!'

Prayer:

Help us, we pray Thee, in spirit and in truth, to come near to the cross of Him who hath redeemed us from death and hell by His death. But we ask also that this morning in coming to the cross, we might then exhibit before Thee a true repentance for sin. It seemed playing when we sinned, but it turns out to be dreadful work, work of the most solemn kind. God forgive us, yea, Thou hast forgiven us! This sacrifice of Christ upon which we do rely is the assurance that Thou hast put away our sin - that we shall not die here.

26

SAVED IN HIS SEAT

'One day as he was teaching, Pharisees and
teachers of the law, who had come from every
village of Galilee and from Judea and Jeru-
salem, were sitting there. And the power of
the Lord was present' (Luke 5:17).

In Victorian times it was quite common for churches to charge 'pew rents' or 'sittings'. Spurgeon eventually abolished them, choosing to live by his book royalties rather than take a salary from 'sittings'.

Many people wanted a 'sitting' just because they knew he was famous or infamous. Some thought he was infamous because of the criticism of him by educated people who ought to have known better. George Eliot, for instance, the pen-name of Mary Ann Cross and author of *The Mill on the Floss* etc, wrote scornfully of Spurgeon in these words: 'This Essex man drove bullock wagons through ecclesiastical aisles; his pulpit gown was a smock-frock'.

It may have been this sort of criticism that made a certain man approach Spurgeon and ask for a regular seat in the Tabernacle. He said rather hesitatingly, 'I may not come up to all that you expect of me, for I have heard that if I take a sitting here you will expect me to be converted, and I cannot guarantee that.' 'I do not want you to guarantee it,' was Spurgeon's reply, 'I do not mean the word, expect, in that sense at all, but I do hope it will be so.'

The man took his sitting and later Spurgeon was able to say, 'And it was so, of course it was so.' The man was converted in the seat that he had rented. As Spurgeon once said, 'There is not a seat in the Tabernacle but somebody has been converted on it.' With 6,000 seats that means 6,000 'pearls' if the seat was used only once. But they were used again and again, and frequently the 'regulars' were asked to go to other churches so that their seats could be occupied by strangers and visitors. Only eternity will reveal the number who were actually converted while sitting in a particular seat in the Tabernacle.

Not only did people offer money for a certain seat, some even offered money to become a Tabernacle member. One man offered Spurgeon £7,000 (which Spurgeon could use for any Tabernacle institution he chose) if only he could become a member. Spurgeon refused it saying that 'if you offered me seventy times seven thousand pounds' he would refuse the man's request.

Prayer:

We would ask, while we stand this morning at the foot of the cross, that we may be crucified with Christ to all the world. Oh that the spear might go through our hearts; that the heart henceforth might be dead to all but Christ. And may hands and feet - the instruments of action and of motion - be fastened to His cross, that we may stray no more, and serve no more the old masters, but may become henceforth wholly the Lord's.

27

A SECOND ROW OF PEARLS

'The twelve gates were twelve pearls, each gate made of a single pearl' (Revelation 21:21).

In a church in Chicago a plea was made for the support of a missionary in the Far West. It appeared that through the reading of Spurgeon's sermons no less than two hundred people had been converted there.

A woman in Scotland tried to burn her Bible and a copy of one of Spurgeon's sermons. Twice the sermon dropped back out of the fire, the second time half-burned and badly scorched. She picked up the remaining readable fragment and was converted through it.

A youth who worked in a newspaper office picked out of the waste paper basket a piece of crumpled paper. It was a page of a sermon by Spurgeon on the Atonement. It led him into new life in Christ.

One woman who was converted through reading one of Spurgeon's sermons bought twenty copies of the same sermon and had them bound into one volume!

Once when preaching in New Park Street Chapel the lights went out. Instead of preaching from his prepared text he spoke in the darkness on a verse that had stood out during the Bible reading. Two people were saved that night.

One woman refused to attend the Tabernacle with her husband but curiosity got the better of her. She dressed in clothes that her husband would not recognise her in but as she pushed her way in through the crowds as Spurgeon was preaching, she heard him say, 'Come in, thou wife of Jeroboam, why feignest thou thyself to be another?' She then attended with her husband and was subsequently saved.

Another Sunday night Spurgeon pointed to the gallery and said, 'Young man, the gloves you have in your pocket are not paid for.' After the service he went to see Spurgeon and begged him not to tell on him. He soon afterwards became a Christian.

At one of his College annual conferences the visiting speaker prayed most earnestly for the children of ministers that they might find Christ while still young. Spurgeon immediately began writing letters to the children of his college men and many testified in later life that they were converted through one of Spurgeon's letters.

A baby cried rather loudly in one of the Tabernacle services. Instead of being irritated or put off Spurgeon prayed for the little life, that he may early come to Christ. The boy was told of it later in life and not only became a Christian but a minister of the gospel.

Prayer:
Lord, save the world, we pray Thee, with the gospel; let it go forth even to the ends thereof. Let these lands know the power of Christ, and the great land across the Atlantic, and that other country on the other side of the world where they dwell of our kith and kin, and every race of man. Oh that Christ might be King of kings openly, as we know He is secretly.

28

SAVED FROM THE SHAKES

*'Do you not know that the wicked will not inherit
the kingdom of God? Do not be deceived: neither
the sexually immoral nor idolaters nor adulterers
nor male prostitutes nor homosexual offenders nor
thieves nor the greedy nor drunkards nor slanderers
nor swindlers will inherit the kingdom of God'
(1 Corinthians 6:10).*

Talking to an American pastor Spurgeon said that
'we usually get what we expect - if we expect fifty
or a hundred conversions a month, the Lord will
not disappoint us. The trouble with us is to bring
our expectations up to the high level of God's
willingness to bestow'. While Spurgeon had great
expectations of conversions through his preaching he could hardly have thought possible the
number who would be saved through his published sermons or other written literature.

For instance, a man had been in Australia for
sixteen years, having emigrated from England.
During that time he had only entered a church
building three times, 'more by accident than de-

sign'. He had also become a drunkard, going 'on the spree' for two or three weeks at a stretch. Twice he suffered from what he called 'the horrors' before being unable to sit, walk, or even lie down because he had an attack of DTs.

Delirium tremens (DTs or The shakes) is a disordered state of mind expressing itself in incoherent speech and is accompanied by hallucinations. Paroxysms of terror are also experienced with violent trembling or shaking.

After one attack of 'the shakes' he picked up a copy of the newspaper. In it was reproduced a copy of a sermon by Spurgeon on The Approachableness of Jesus. He began reading it but before he had got very far he could not see the print for tears, tears of shame. He had to shield his eyes with his hands.

Soon he was able to begin reading again and within a short while he was looking to Jesus to be relieved of his burden of sin and shame.

The *delirium tremens* began to subside and then vanished 'like a heavy dew on a summer's morning'. Although he was still bodily weak as a consequence of his recent long drinking-bout, he felt well and healthy mentally and spiritually, enjoying peace such as he had never felt in his life before.

Some years later, when Spurgeon's son Tom

went to Australia the man saved from the shakes
went to see him and showed him the actual newspaper sermon by his father that had been the means
of his becoming one of Spurgeon's 'pearls'.

Prayer:

We would take the cup of salvation and call
upon the name of the Lord. We would pay
our vows now in the midst of all the Lord's
people and in the courts of His house; and
this is a part payment of our vow that we
bless the Lord Jesus who hath put away our
sin. We bless Him that He hath redeemed us
unto Himself not with corruptible things as
silver and gold, but with His own
precious blood; and we do avow ourselves
today to be the Lord's.

29

A PARALYTIC PEARL

*'As Peter travelled about the country, he went to
visit the saints in Lydda. There he found a man
named Aeneas, a paralytic who had been bedridden
for eight years. Aeneas, Peter said to him, Jesus
Christ heals you' (Acts 9:32-34).*

He lived quite near the Tabernacle but was unable
to get there. He was in a wheelchair and had been
so for over twelve months. He had not been so
terribly wicked during his former active life;
'careless' was how he put it. 'I know I have done
wrong; for I have often worked on Sundays, when
I might have been at a place of worship'.

He was visited fairly frequently by a London
City Missionary who added that the man was
'rather self-righteous', especially when he tried to
explain the way of salvation to him and persuade
him to become a Christian. One wonders whether
he would have counted his Sunday work a sin in
this twentieth century, instead of Victorian times,
when so many supermarkets and other chain stores

are openly flouting the law with their Sunday trading!

One day when the City missionary called he found the man more anxious about his soul's salvation. He had been reading *The Daily News* and offered to read a piece in it to the missionary. He said that he found it 'just for me'. It happened to be an extract from a sermon by C H Spurgeon, the preacher he could not go to hear, even if he had wanted to, because of his paralysis. Spurgeon's text was: 'He knoweth the way that I take; when he hath tried me, I shall come forth as gold'.

The paper was the other side of the room so the City Missionary got it for him and he read the extract over and over again out loud. Then he said, 'It is every word for me'. God blessed it to him not only for his salvation but he saw his physical affliction in a new light. He accepted his paralysis and knew that God had used it for his eternal good. He 'fully trusted Jesus', as the City Missionary put it, and since he could not get to the Tabernacle began to read a volume of Spurgeon's sermons, declaring again and again that 'Every word goes to my heart'.

Oh yes, the newspaper was passed on to him by the publican who kept a public house next door!

Spurgeon, when he heard of this 'pearl', included his testimony in the Notes that he used to write in his church magazine *The Sword and the Trowel*. Thus the man's witness to the saving power of the gospel was not confined to the few visitors who came to his humble home but to the thousands all over the world who waited with eager anticipation for the magazine's appearance month by month. Spurgeon's final comment at the end of his note in *The Sword and the Trowel* was: 'God works in his own way when he wants to save a soul'.

Prayer:
There are those that have dear ones very sick and ill: the Lord comfort and sustain them under great trouble of seeing others suffer. Remember any that are in temporal difficulties, and those who are themselves ill. There are among Thine own people plants that grow in the shade. Remember the man of a sorrowful spirit, and the woman of a sad heart. Lift up the light of Thy countenance upon Thy people.

30

SAVED BY A SON'S GUILE

'I am sending you out like sheep among
wolves. Therefore be as shrewd as snakes
and as innocent as doves' (Matthew 10:16).

People arranging a rendezvous in London often
agree to meet at a main line station 'beneath the
station clock in the foyer'. Others may say, 'Outside the town hall' or some other well-known,
public building.

During Spurgeon's ministry at the Tabernacle
there lived a man who grew to hate the very name
of Spurgeon. This was not from any personal
knowledge of the great preacher, for he had never
met him or even heard him. He was very preju-
diced against 'dissenters' as nonconformists or
freechurchmen were then referred to. Spurgeon
he regarded as the worst dissenter of them all.

The man's son was converted to Christ and a
little while afterwards decided to go to London to
find employment. A few weeks later his father
came up to London to see how the son was doing.

Knowing he was coming the son arranged to meet his father outside Spurgeon's Tabernacle. Since he had now started work the only free time he had to meet his father was on Sunday morning. The son chose a time when he knew the people would be going into the Tabernacle for the Sunday morning service.

As he guessed, his father was intrigued by the vast crowd of people flocking to get into the Tabernacle to hear Spurgeon. He could not resist the temptation; his curiosity got the better of him; he suggested to his son that they too went in.

The father was passionately fond of singing and during the opening hymn, 'All hail the power of Jesus' name', he broke down and wept. His heart was now softened to listen to Spurgeon preach on the text, 'Deep calleth unto deep'. Although he was not converted there and then, he was so impressed by the sermon that he bought several copies of it when they appeared the next week in print and gave them to his friends and neighbours.

His estimation of Spurgeon soared. Just as he had regarded him as 'the very worst' (of dissenters), now he was 'the very best' (of preachers).

During his reading of *The Metropolitan Tabernacle Pulpit* series he became a Christian, the sermons then becoming his weekly spiritual food, and when he died some time later he passed away assuring relatives and friends that he had no fear of death.

A son's guile, the singing of a well-known hymn, a spoken and a printed sermon - all these were used by God the Holy Spirit to bring a man to the feet of the Saviour.

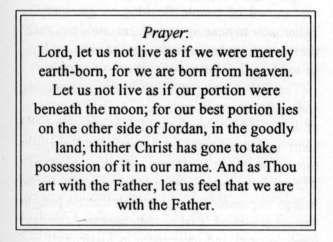

Prayer:
Lord, let us not live as if we were merely earth-born, for we are born from heaven.
Let us not live as if our portion were beneath the moon; for our best portion lies on the other side of Jordan, in the goodly land; thither Christ has gone to take possession of it in our name. And as Thou art with the Father, let us feel that we are with the Father.

31

THE PEARL OF PEARLS

Spurgeon's account of his own conversion[1]

'Look unto me, and be ye saved, all the ends of the earth: for I am God, and there is none else' (Isaiah 45:22 AV, as this is the version Spurgeon would have heard it in).

'It is about twenty-six years ago - twenty-six years exactly last Thursday - that I looked unto the Lord, and found salvation through this text. You have often heard me tell how I had been wandering about, seeking rest, and finding none, till a plain, unlettered, lay preacher among the Primitive Methodists stood up in the pulpit, and gave out this passage as his text: 'Look unto me, and be ye saved, all the ends of the earth'. He had not much

---

[1] Spurgeon preached three times on Isaiah 45:22, the text that was the means of his conversion. Each time he gave his testimony in his own words. Besides that, his conversion is described, on average, five times in every volume of sermons. (See *Searchlight on Spurgeon*, E W Hayden, for more details of Spurgeon's conversion.)

to say, thank God, for that compelled him to keep on repeating his text, and there was nothing needed - by me, at any rate - except his text. I remember how he said, "It is Christ that speaks. I am in the garden in an agony, pouring out my soul unto death; I am on the tree, dying for sinners; look unto me! look unto me! That is all you have to do. A child can look. One who is almost an idiot can look. However weak, or however poor, a man may be, he can look; and if he looks, the promise is that he shall live".

'Then, stopping, he pointed to where I was sitting under the gallery and he said, "That young man there looks very miserable". I expect I did, for that is how I felt. Then he said, "There is no hope for you, young man, or any chance of getting rid of your sin, but by looking to Jesus"; and he shouted, as I think only a Primitive Methodist can, "Look! young man! Look now!" And I did look; and when they sang a hallelujah before they went home, in their own earnest way, I am sure I joined in it.

'It happened to be a day when the snow was lying deep, and more was falling; so, as I went home, those words of David kept ringing through my heart: Wash me, and I shall be whiter than snow; and it seemed as if all nature was in accord with that blessed deliverance from sin which I had found in a single moment by looking to Jesus.

'I have always inclined, when this time of the year comes round (January), to preach from this text. I have sometimes thought, "They will suppose I must go over the same ground again, and give them the same sermon; and so, perhaps, I shall not have so attentive an audience". I cannot help it if it is so, for I must preach from this text. As it was blessed to me, I hope it will be blessed to somebody else.'

'LOOK UNTO ME, AND BE YE SAVED, ALL THE ENDS OF THE EARTH: FOR I AM GOD, AND THERE IS NONE ELSE.'

Prayer:

Oh, what Thou hast done for us, great God! What a wondrous grace is this; and what hast Thou prepared for us? Who can tell what Thou hast laid up for them that fear Thee, among the sons of men. We would approach Thee with that filial boldness which is born of a sense of love, and daily grows upon mercies perpetually given. We love Thee; we trust Thee; we delight in Thee; Thou art all in all to us. Thou hast made with us an everlasting Covenant, ordered in all things and sure; and therefore we are bound to Thee by bonds that never can be broken.

32

SOUL WINNING [1]

'He that winneth souls is wise' (Proverbs 11:30)

The text does not say, 'He that winneth sovereigns is wise', though no doubt he thinks himself wise, and perhaps, in a certain grovelling sense in these days of competition, he must be so; but such wisdom is of the earth, and ends with the earth; and there is another world where the currencies of Europe will not be accepted, nor their past possession be any sign of wealth or wisdom.

Solomon, in the text before us, awards no crown for wisdom to crafty statesmen, or even to the ablest of rulers; he issues no diplomas even to philosophers, poets, or men of wit; he crowns with laurel only those who win souls. He does not declare that he who preaches is necessarily wise - and alas! there are multitudes who preach, and gain much applause and eminence, who win no souls, and who shall find it go hard with them at the last, because in all probability they have run and the Master has never sent them. He does not say that he who talks about winning souls is wise,

1. A Sermon delivered by C H Spurgeon at the Metropolitan Tabernacle, Newington

since to lay down rules for others is a very simple thing, but to carry them out one's self is far more difficult.

He who actually, really, and truly turns men from the error of their ways to God, and so is made the means of saving them from going down to hell, is a wise man; and that is true of him whatever his style of soul-winning may be. He may be a Paul, deeply logical, profound in doctrine, able to command all candid judgments; and if he thus win souls he is wise. He may be an Apollos, grandly rhetorical, whose lofty genius soars into the very heaven of eloquence; and if he wins souls in that way he is wise, but not otherwise. Or he may be a Cephas, rough and rugged, using uncouth metaphor and stern declamation, but if he win souls he is no less wise than his polished brother or his argumentative friend, but not else.

The great wisdom of soul-winners, according to the text, is proven only by their actual success in really winning souls. To their own Master they are accountable for the ways in which they go to work, not to us. Do not let us be comparing and contrasting this minister and that. Who art thou that judgest another man's servants? Wisdom is justified in all her children. Only children wrangle about incidental methods: men look at sublime results. Do these workers of many sorts and divers manners win souls? Then they are wise; and you who criticise them, being yourselves unfruitful, cannot be wise, even though you affect to be their judges. God proclaims soul-winners to be wise, dispute it who dare. This degree from the College of Heaven may surely stand them in good stead, let their fellow mortals say what they will of them.

'He that winneth souls is wise', and this can be seen very clearly. He must be a wise man in even ordinary respects who can by grace achieve so divine a marvel. Great soul-winners never have been fools. A man whom God qualifies to win souls could probably do anything else which providence might allot him.

Take Martin Luther! Why, sirs, the man was not only fit to work a Reformation, but he could have ruled a nation or have commanded an army. Think of Whitefield, and remember that the thundering eloquence which stirred all England was not associated with a weak judgment, or an absence of brain-power; the man was a master-orator, and if he had addicted himself to commerce would have taken a chief place amongst the merchants, or had he been a politician, amid admiring senates would have commanded the listening ear. He that winneth souls is usually a man who could have done anything else if God had called him to it.

I know the Lord uses what means he wills, but he always uses means suitable to the end; and if you tell me that David slew Goliath with a sling,

I answer - it was the best weapon in the world to reach so tall a giant, and the very fittest weapon that David could have used, for he had been skilled in it from his youth up. There is always an adaptation in the instruments which God uses to produce the ordained result, and though the glory is not to them, nor the excellence in them, but all is to be ascribed to God, yet is there a fitness and preparedness which God seeth, even if we do not. It is assuredly true that soul-winners are by no means idiots or simpletons, but such as God maketh wise for himself, though vainglorious wiseacres may dub them fools.

'He that winneth souls is wise', because he has selected a wise object. I think it was Michael Angelo who once carved certain magnificent statues in snow. They are gone; the material readily compacted by the frost as readily melted in the heat. Far wiser was he when he fashioned the enduring marble, and produced works which will last all down the ages. But even marble itself is consumed and fretted by the tooth of time; and he is wise who selects for his raw material immortal souls, whose existence shall outlast the stars. If God shall bless us to the winning of souls, our work shall remain when the wood, and hay, and stubble of earth's art and science shall have gone to the dust from which they sprang. In heaven itself, the soul-winner, blessed of God, shall have memorials of his work preserved for ever in the galleries of the skies.

He has selected a wise object, for what can be wiser than to glorify God, and what, next to that, can be wiser than in the highest sense to bless our fellow men; to snatch a soul from the gulf that yawns, to lift it up to the heaven that glorifies; to deliver an immortal from the thralldom of Satan, and to bring him into the liberty of Christ? What more excellent than this? I say, that such an aim would commend itself to all right minds, and that angels themselves may envy us poor sons of men that we are permitted to make this our life-object, to win souls for Jesus Christ. Wisdom herself assents to the excellence of the design.

To accomplish such a work, a man must be wise, for to win a soul requires infinite wisdom. God himself wins not souls without wisdom, for the eternal plan of salvation was dictated by an infallible judgment, and in every line of it infinite skill is apparent. Christ, God's great soul-winner, is 'the wisdom of God', as well as 'the power of God'. There is as much wisdom to be seen in the new creation as in the old. In a sinner saved, there is as much of God to be beheld as in a universe rising out of nothing; and we, then, who are to be workers together with God, proceeding side by side with him to the great work of soul-winning, must be wise too. It is a work which filled a

Saviour's heart - a work which moved the Eternal mind or ever the earth was. It is no child's play, nor a thing to be achieved while we are half asleep, nor to be attempted without deep consideration, nor to be carried on without gracious help from the only-wise God, our Saviour. The pursuit is wise.

Mark ye well, my brethren, that he who is successful in soul-winning, will prove to have been a wise man in the judgment of those who see the end as well as the beginning.

Even if I were utterly selfish, and had no care for anything but my own happiness, I would choose, if I might, under God, to be a soul-winner, for never did I know perfect, overflowing, unutterable happiness of the purest and most ennobling order, till I first heard of one who had sought and found a Saviour through my means. I recollect the thrill of joy which went through me! No young mother ever rejoiced so much over her first-born child - no warrior was so exultant over a hard-won victory. Oh! the joy of knowing that a sinner once at enmity has been reconciled to God, by the Holy Spirit, through the words spoken by our feeble lips. Since then, by grace given to me, the thought of which prostrates me in self-abasement, I have seen and heard of, not hundreds only, but even thousands of sinners turned from the error of their ways by the testimony of God in me.

Let afflictions come, let trials be multiplied as

God willeth, still this joy preponderates above all others, the joy that we are unto God a sweet savour of Christ in every place, and that as often as we preach the Word, hearts are unlocked, bosoms heave with a new life, eyes weep for sin, and their tears are wiped away as they see the great Substitute for sin, and live.

Beyond all controversy, it is a joy worth worlds to win souls, and, thank God, it is a joy that does not cease with this mortal life. It must be no small bliss to hear, as one wings his flight up to the eternal throne, the wings of others fluttering at one's side towards the same glory, and turning round and questioning them, to hear them say, 'We are entering with you through the gates of pearl; you brought us to the Saviour'. To be welcomed to the skies by those who call us father in God - father in better bonds than those of earth, father through grace and sire for immortality. It will be bliss beyond compare to meet in yon eternal seats with those begotten of us in Christ Jesus, for whom we travailed in birth, till Christ was formed in them, the hope of glory. This is to have many heavens - a heaven in every one won for Christ according to the Master's promise, 'they that turn many to righteousness, shall shine as the stars for ever and ever'.

I have said enough, brethren, I trust, to make some of you desire to occupy the position of soul-winners: but before I further address myself to my text, I should like to remind you, that the honour does not belong to ministers only; they may take their full share of it, but it belongs to every one of you who have devoted yourselves to Christ: such honour have all the saints.

Every man here, every woman here, every child here, whose heart is right with God, may be a soul-winner. There is no man placed by God's providence where he cannot do some good. There is not a glowworm under a hedge, but gives a needed light; and there is not a labouring man, a suffering woman, a servant-girl, a chimney-sweeper, or a crossing-sweeper, but what has opportunities for serving God; and what I have said of soul-winners, belongs not to the learned doctor of divinity, or to the eloquent preacher alone, but to you all who are in Christ Jesus. You can each of you, if grace enable you, be thus wise, and win the happiness of turning souls to Christ through the Holy Spirit.

I am about to dwell upon my text in this way: 'He that winneth souls is wise'; I shall, first, make that fact stand out a little clearer by explaining the metaphor used in the text - winning souls; and then, secondly, by giving you some lessons in the matter of soul-winning, through which I trust the conviction will be forced upon each believing mind that the work needs the highest wisdom.

1. First, LET US CONSIDER THE METAPHOR USED IN THE TEXT - 'He that winneth souls is wise'.

We use the word 'win' in many ways. It is sometimes found in very bad company, in those games of chance, juggling tricks and sleight-of-hand, or thimble-rigging (to use a plain word), which sharpers are so fond of winning by.

I am sorry to say that much of legerdemain[1] and trickery are to be met within the religious world. Why, there are those who pretend to save souls by curious tricks, intricate manoeuvres, and dexterous posture making. A basin of water, half-a-dozen drops, certain syllables - heigh, presto! - the infant is a child of grace, and becomes a member of Christ and an inheritor of the kingdom of heaven. This aqueous regeneration surpasses my belief; it is a trick which I do not understand: the initiated only can perform the beautiful piece of magic, which excels anything ever attempted by the Wizard of the North[2].

There is a way, too, of winning souls by laying hands upon heads, only the elbows of aforesaid hands must be encased in lawn[3], and then the machinery acts, and there is grace conferred by blessed fingers! I must confess I do not understand the occult science, but at this need not wonder, for

1. Slight of hand or juggling. 2. From Sir Walter Scott's writings on Demonology and Witchcraft. 3. Fine linen, used especially of bishops' sleeves.

the profession of saving souls by such juggling can only be carried out by certain favoured persons who have received apostolic succession direct from Judas Iscariot. This episcopal confirmation, when men pretend that it confers grace, is an infamous piece of juggling.

The whole thing is an abomination. Only to think that in this nineteenth century there should be men who preach up salvation by sacraments, and salvation by themselves forsooth! Why, sirs, it is surely too late in the day to come to us with this drivel!

Priestcraft, let us hope, is an anachronism, and the sacramental theory out of date. These things might have done for those who could not read, and for the days when books were scarce, but ever since the day when the glorious Luther was helped by God to proclaim with thunder-claps the emancipating truth, 'By grace are ye saved, through faith, and that not of yourselves, it is the gift of God', there has been too much light for these Popish owls. Let them go back to their ivy-mantled towers, and complain to the moon of those who spoiled of old their kingdom of darkness. Let shaven crowns go to Bedlam, and scarlet hats to the scarlet harlot, but let not Englishmen yield them respect. Modern Tractarianism is a bastard Popery, too mean, too shifty, too double-dealing to delude men of honest minds.

If we win souls it shall be by other arts than Jesuits and shavelings[1] can teach us. Trust not in any man who pretends to priesthood. Priests are liars by trade, and deceivers by profession. We cannot save souls in their theatrical way, and do not want to do so, for we know that with such jugglery as that, Satan will hold the best hand, and laugh at priests as he turns the cards against them at the last.

How do we win souls, then? Why, the word 'win' has a better meaning far. It is used in *warfare*. Warriors win cities and provinces.

Now, to win a soul, is a much more difficult thing than to win a city. Observe the earnest soul-winner at his work; how cautiously he seeks his great Captain's directions to know when to hang out the white flag to invite the heart to surrender to the sweet love of a dying Saviour; when, at the proper time, to hang out the black flag of threatening, showing that if grace be not received, judgment will surely follow; and when to unfurl, with dread reluctance, the red flag of the terrors of God against stubborn, impenitent souls.

The soul-winner has to sit down before a soul as a great captain before a walled town; to draw his lines of circumvallation, to cast up his entrench-

---

1. A lad. In 1348 when the clergy were dying fast because of the Black Death, youths were admitted to holy orders by being shaven. The word came later to mean a friar or priest.

ments and fix his batteries. He must not advance too fast - he may overdo the fighting; he must not move too slowly, for he may seem not to be in earnest, and may do mischief. Then he must know which gate to attack - how to plant his guns at Eargate, and how to discharge them; how, sometimes, to keep the batteries going, day and night, with red-hot shot, if perhaps he may make a breach in the walls; at other times, to lay by and cease, and then, on a sudden, to open all the batteries with terrific violence, if peradventure he may take the soul by surprise or cast in a truth when it was not expected, to burst like a shell in the soul, and do damage to the dominions of sin.

The Christian soldier must know how to advance by little and little - to sap that prejudice, to undermine that old enmity, to blow into the air that lust, and at the last, to storm the citadel. It is his to throw the scaling ladder up, and to have his ears gladdened as he hears a clicking on the wall of the heart, telling that the scaling ladder has grasped and has gained firm hold; and then, with his sabre between his teeth, to climb up, and spring on the man, and slay his unbelief in the name of God, and capture the city, and run up the blood-red flag of the cross of Christ, and say, 'The heart is won, won for Christ at last.'

This needs a warrior well trained - a master in his art. After many days' attack, many weeks of waiting, many an hour of storming by prayer and battering by entreaty, to carry the Malakoff [1] of depravity, this is the work, this the difficulty. It takes no fool to do this. God's grace must make a man wise thus to capture Mansoul, to lead its captivity captive, and open wide the heart's gates that the Prince Immanuel may come in. This is winning a soul.

The word 'win' was commonly used among the ancients, *to signify winning in the wrestling match*.

When the Greek sought to win the laurel, or the ivy crown, he was compelled a long time before to put himself through a course of training, and when he came forth at last stripped for the encounter, he had no sooner exercised himself in the first few efforts than you saw how every muscle and every nerve had been developed in him. He had a stern opponent, and he knew it, and therefore left none of his energy unused. While the wrestling was going on you could see the man's eye, how he watched every motion, every feint of his antagonist, and how his hand, his foot, and his whole body were thrown into the encounter. He feared to

1. In 1831, a sailor and ropemaker named Alexander Malakoff lived in Sebastopol. He was dismissed from his job in the dockyard for rioting and opened a liquor shop, calling the shop after himself. Houses sprang up around his shop until quite a township developed. It became fortified with a Malakoff Tower that became famous in the Crimean War.

meet with a fall: he hoped to give one to his foe.

Now, a true soul-winner has often to come to close quarters with the devil within men. He has to struggle with their prejudice, with their love of sin, with their unbelief, with their pride, and then again, all of a sudden, to grapple with their despair; at one moment he strives with their self-righteousness, at the next moment with their unbelief in God. Ten thousand arts are used to prevent the soul-winner from being conqueror in the encounter, but if God has sent him he will never renounce his hold of the soul he seeks till he has given a throw to the power of sin, and won another soul for Christ.

Besides that, there is another meaning to the word 'win', upon which I cannot expatiate here. We use the word, you know, in a softer sense than these which have been mentioned, *when we come to deal with hearts*.

There are secret and mysterious ways by which those who love win the object of their affection, which are wise in their fitness to the purpose. I cannot tell you how the lover wins his fond one, but experience has probably taught you. The weapon of this warfare is not always the same, yet where that victory is won the wisdom of the means becomes clear to every eye. The weapon of love is sometimes a look, or a soft word whispered and eagerly listened to; sometimes it is a tear; but this I know, that we have, most of us in our turn, cast around another heart a chain which that other would not care to break, and which has linked us twain in a blessed captivity which has cheered our life.

Yes, and that is very nearly the way in which we have to save souls. That illustration is nearer the mark than any of the others. Love is the true way of soul-winning, for when I spoke of storming the walls, and when I spoke of wrestling, those were but metaphors, but this is near the fact. We win by love.

We win hearts for Jesus by love, by sympathy with their sorrow, by anxiety lest they should perish, by pleading with God for them with all our hearts that they should not be left to die unsaved, by pleading with them for God that, for their own sake, they would seek mercy and find grace. Yes, sirs, there is a spiritual wooing and winning of hearts for the Lord Jesus; and if you would learn the way, you must ask God to give you a tender heart and a sympathising soul. I believe that much of the secret of soul-winning lies in having bowels of compassion, in having spirits that can be touched with the feeling of human infirmities. Carve a preacher out of granite, and even if you give him an angel's tongue, he will convert nobody. Put him into the most fashionable pulpit, make his elocution faultless, and his matter profoundly orthodox, but so long as he bears within his bosom a hard heart he can never win a soul.

Soul-saving requires a heart that beats hard against the ribs. It requires a soul full of the milk of human kindness; this is the *sine qua non* of success. This is the chief natural qualification for a soul-winner, which, under God and blessed of him, will accomplish wonders.

I have not looked at the Hebrew of the text, but I find - and you will find who have margins to your Bibles - that it is, 'He that *taketh* souls is wise' which word refers to fishing, or to bird-catching. Every Sunday when I leave my house, I cannot help seeing as I come along, men, with their little cages and their stuffed birds, trying all around the common, and in the fields, to catch poor little warblers. They understand the method of alluring and entrapping their little victims. Soul-winners might learn much from them. We must have our lures for souls adapted to attract, to fascinate, to grasp. We must go forth with our bird-lime, our decoys, our nets, our baits, so that we may but catch the souls of men. Their enemy is a fowler possessed of the basest and most astounding cunning; we must outwit him with the guile of honesty, the craft of grace. But the art is to be learned only by divine teaching, and herein we must be wise and willing to learn.

The man who takes fish, must also have some art in him. Washington Irving, I think it is, tells us of some three gentlemen who had read in Izaak

Walton all about the delights of fishing. So they must needs enter upon the same amusement, and accordingly they become disciples of the gentle art. They went into New York and bought the best rods and lines that could be purchased, and they found out the exact fly for the particular day or month, so that the fish might bite at once, and as it were fly into the basket with alacrity. They fished, and fished, and fished the live-long day, but the basket was empty. They were getting disgusted with a sport that had no sport in it, when a ragged boy came down from the hills, without shoes or stockings, and humiliated them to the last degree. He had a bit of a bough pulled from off a tree, and a piece of string, and a bent pin; he put a worm on it, threw it in, and out came a fish directly, as if it were a needle drawn to a magnet. In again went the line, and out came another fish, and so on, till his basket was quite full. They asked him how he did it. Ah! he said, he could not tell them that, but it was easy enough when you had the way of it.

Much the same is it in fishing for men. Some preachers who have silk lines and fine rods, preach very eloquently and exceedingly gracefully, but they never win souls. I know not how it is, but another man comes, with very simple language, but with a warm heart, and, straightway, men are converted to God. Surely there must be a sympathy between the minister and the souls he would win. God gives to those whom he makes soul-winners a natural love to their work, and a spiritual fitness for it. There is a sympathy between those who are to be blessed and those who are to be the means of blessing, and very much by this sympathy, under God, souls are taken; but it is as clear as noonday, that to be a fisher of men a man must be wise. 'He that winneth souls is wise.'

2. And now, brethren and sisters, you who are engaged in the Lord's work from week to week, and who seek to win men's souls to Christ, I am, in the second place, to illustrate this BY TELLING YOU OF SOME OF THE WAYS BY WHICH SOULS ARE TO BE WON.

The preacher himself wins souls, I believe, best, when he believes in the reality of his work, when he believes in instantaneous conversions.

How can he expect God to do what he does not believe God will do? *He succeeds best who expects conversion every time he preaches.* According to his faith so shall it be done unto him. To be content without conversions is the surest way never to have them: to drive with a single aim entirely at the saving of souls is the surest method of usefulness. If we sigh and cry till men are saved, saved they will be.

He will succeed best, *who keeps closest to soul-saving truth.*

Now, all truth is not soul-saving, though all

truth may be edifying. He that keeps to the simple story of the cross, tells men over and over again that whosoever believeth in Christ is not condemned, that to be saved, nothing is wanted but a simple trust in the crucified Redeemer; he whose ministry is much made up of the glorious story of the cross, the sufferings of the dying Lamb, the mercy of God, the willingness of the great Father to receive returning prodigals; he who cries, in fact, from day to day, 'Behold the Lamb of God, which taketh away the sin of the world', he is likely to be a soul-winner, especially if he adds to this much prayer for souls, much anxious desire that men may be brought to Jesus, and then in his private life seeks as much as in his public ministry to be telling out to others of the love of the dear Saviour of men.

But I am not talking to ministers, but to you who sit in the pew, and therefore to you let me turn myself more directly. Brothers and sisters, you have different gifts. I hope you use them all. Perhaps some of you, though members of the church, think you have none; but every believer has his gift, and his portion of work. What can you do to win souls?

Let me recommend to those who think they can do nothing, *the bringing of others to hear the word*.

That is a duty much neglected. I can hardly ask you to bring anybody here, but many of you attend other places which are not perhaps half filled. Fill them. Do not grumble at the small congregation, but make it larger. Take somebody with you to the very next sermon, and at once the congregation will be increased. Go up with the prayer that your minister's sermon may be blessed, and if you cannot preach yourselves, yet, by bringing others under the sound of the word, you may be doing what is next best. This is a very commonplace and simple remark, but let me press it upon you, for it is of great practical value.

Many churches and chapels which are almost empty, might soon have large audiences if those who profit by the word would tell others about the profit they have received, and induce them to attend the same ministry.

Especially in this London of ours, where so many will not go up to the house of God - persuade your neighbours to come forth to the place of worship; look after them; make them feel that it is a wrong thing to stop at home on the Sunday from morning till night. I do not say upbraid them, that does little good; but I do say entice them, persuade them. Let them have your tickets for the Taber-nacle, for instance, sometimes, or stand in the aisles yourself, and let them have your seat. Get them under the word, and who knoweth what may be the result? Oh, what a blessing it would be to you if you heard that what you could not do, for you could scarcely speak for Christ, was done by your pastor, by the power of the Holy Spirit, through your inducing one to come within gun-shot of the gospel!

Next to that, soul-winners, *try after sermon to talk to strangers*.

The preacher may have missed the mark - you need not miss it; or the preacher may have struck the mark, and you can help to make the impression deeper by a kind word. I recollect several persons joining the church who traced their conversion to the ministry in the Surrey Music Hall, but who said it was not that alone, but another agency cooperating therewith. They were fresh from the country, and some good man, I knew him well, I think he is in heaven now, met two of them at the gate, spoke to them, said he hoped they had enjoyed what they had heard; heard their answer; asked them if they were coming in the evening; said he would be glad if they would drop into his house to tea; they did, and he had a word with them about the Master. The next Sunday it was the same, and at last, those whom the sermons had not much impressed, were brought to hear with other ears, till by-and-by, through the good old man's persuasive words, and the good Lord's gracious work, they were converted to God.

There is a fine hunting-ground here, and indeed in every large congregation for you who really want to do good. How many come into this house every morning and evening with no thought about receiving Christ. Oh! if you would all help me, you who love the Master, if you would all help me by speaking to your neighbours who sit near to you, how much might be accomplished! Never let anybody say, 'I came to the Tabernacle three months, and nobody spoke to me', but do, by a sweet familiarity, which ought always to be allowable in the house of God, seek with your whole heart to impress upon your friends the truth which I can only put into the ear, but which God may help you to put into the heart.

Further, let me commend to you, dear friends, *the art of buttonholing acquaintances and relatives*.

If you cannot preach to a hundred, preach to one. Get a hold of the man alone, and in love, quietly and prayerfully, talk to him; 'One!' say you. Well, is not one enough? I know your ambition, young man; you want to preach here, to these thousands; be content and begin with the ones. Your Master was not ashamed to sit on the well and preach to one, and when he had finished his sermon he had really done good to all the city of Samaria, for that one woman became a missionary to her friends.

Timidity often prevents our being useful in this direction, but we must not give way to it; it must not be tolerated that Christ should be unknown through our silence, and sinners unwarned through our negligence. We must school and train ourselves to deal personally with the unconverted. We must not excuse ourselves, but force ourselves to the irksome task till it becomes easy. This is one of the most honourable modes of soul-winning, and if it requires more than ordinary zeal and courage, so much the more reason for our resolving to master it. Beloved, we must win souls, we cannot live and see men damned; we must have them brought to Jesus. Oh! then be up and doing, and let none around you die unwarned, unwept, uncared for. A tract is a useful thing, but a living word is better. Your eye, and face, and voice will all help. Do not be so cowardly as to give a piece of paper where your own speech would be so much better. I charge you, attend to this, for Jesus' sake.

Some of you could write letters for your Lord and Master.

To far-off friends a few loving lines may be most influential for good. Be like the men of Issachar, who handled the pen. Paper and ink are never better used than in soul-winning. Much has been done by this method. Could not you do it? Will you not try?

Some of you, at any rate, if you could not speak or write much, *could live much.*

That is a fine way of preaching, that of preaching with your feet, I mean preaching by your life, and conduct, and conversation. That loving wife who weeps in secret over an infidel husband, but is always so kind to him; that dear child whose heart is broken with a father's blasphemy, but is so much more obedient than he used to be before conversion; that servant whom the master swears at, but whom he could trust with his purse, and the gold uncounted in it; that man in trade who is sneered at as a Presbyterian, but who, nevertheless, is straight as a line, and would not be compelled to do a dirty action, no, not for all the mint; these are the men and women who preach the best sermons; these are your practical preachers. Give us your holy living, and with your holy living as the leverage, we will move the world. Under God's blessing we will find tongues, if we can, but we need greatly the lives of our people to illustrate what our tongues have to say.

The gospel is something like an illustrated paper. The preacher's words are the letterpress, but the pictures are the living men and women who form our churches; and as when people take up such a newspaper, they very often do not read the letterpress, but they always look at the pictures - so in a church, outsiders may not come to hear the preacher, but they always consider, observe, and criticise the lives of the members. If you would be soul-winners, then, dear brethren and sisters, see that you live the gospel. I have no greater joy than this, that my children walk in the truth.

One thing more, *the soul-winner must be a master of the art of prayer*.

You cannot bring souls to God if you go not to God yourself. You must get your battle-axe, and your weapons of war, from the armoury of sacred communion with Christ. If you are much alone with Jesus, you will catch his Spirit; you will be fired with the flame that burned in his breast, and consumed his life. You will weep with the tears that fell upon Jerusalem when he saw it perishing, and if you cannot speak so eloquently as he did, yet shall there be about what you say somewhat of the same power which in him thrilled the hearts and awoke the consciences of men.

My dear hearers, specially you members of the church, I am always so anxious lest any of you should begin to lie upon your oars, and take things easy in the matters of God's kingdom. There are some of you - I bless you, and I bless God at the remembrance of you - who are in season, and out of season, in earnest for winning souls, and you are the truly wise: but I fear there are others whose hands are slack, who are satisfied to let me preach, but do not preach themselves; who take these seats and occupy these pews, and hope the cause goes well, but that is all they do.

Oh, do let me see you all in earnest! A great host of four thousand members - for that is now as nearly as possible the accurate counting of our numbers - what ought we not to do if we are all alive, and all in earnest! *But such a host, without the spirit of enthusiasm*, becomes a mere mob, an unwieldy mass, out of which mischief grows, and no good results arise. If you were all firebrands for Christ, you might set the nation on a blaze. If you were all wells of living water, how many thirsty souls might drink and be refreshed!

One thing more you can do. If some of you feel you cannot do much personally, *you can always help the College*, and there it is that we find tongues for the dumb. Our young men are called out by God to preach; we give them some little education and training, and then away they go to Australia, to Canada, to the islands of the sea, to Scotland, to Wales, and throughout England, preaching the Word; and it is often, it must be often, a consolation to some of you, to think that if you have not spoken with your own tongues as you could desire, you have at least spoken by the tongues of others, so that through you the word of God has been sounded abroad throughout all this region.

Beloved, there is one question I will ask, and I have done, and that is, *Are your own souls won*? You cannot win others else. Are you yourselves saved? My hearers, every one of you, under that gallery there, and you behind here, are you yourselves saved?

What if this night you should have to answer that question to another and greater than I am? What if the bony finger of the last great orator should be uplifted instead of mine? What if his unconquerable eloquence should turn those bones to stone, and glaze those eyes, and make the blood chill in your veins? Could you hope, in your last extremity, that you were saved? If not saved, how will you ever be?

The way to be saved is simply to trust in what the Son of man did when he became man, and suffered the punishment for all those who trust him. For all his people, Christ was a substitute. His people are those who trust him. If you trust him, he was punished for your sins; and you cannot be punished for them, for God cannot punish sin twice, first in Christ, and then in you. If you trust Jesus, who now liveth at the right hand of God, you are this moment pardoned, and you shall for ever be saved.

O that you would trust him now! Perhaps it may be now or never with you. May it be now, even now, and then, trusting in Jesus, dear friends, you will have no need to hesitate when the question is asked, 'Are you saved?' for you can answer, 'Ay, that I am, for it is written, He that believeth in him is not condemned.' Trust him, then, trust him now, and then God help you to be a soul-winner, and you shall be wise, and God shall be glorified.

"Bipolar disorder can be a confusing, even scary thing to a child. This charming book does a great job explaining it to young readers, and leaves plenty of room open for discussion."
— *Lloyd Jones, author of*
The Princess and the Fog

"This is a very good book — I really liked it. All secondary schools should have a copy in their library, along with other books to help children if they notice their parents or carers are acting a bit differently than they have in the past. I feel it is a book that incorporated a story with interesting facts. Some children could understand the situation; it could be real life for them and they could relate to it. I highly recommend the book to every child as it will inform them on elements of the real world."
— *Alessandro (aged 11), who has friends affected by mental ill health and wants to be able to help*

"This book gives hope and is realistic. It gives children and young people a tool to ask for support; it increases their autonomy and offers them a language to explain their experiences. I especially like the recommendations for friends and school. The book is relatable across experiences; it gives a simple explanation or space for wider discussion."
— *Claire James, social worker supporting vulnerable children and young people*

04511423